MADISON SQUARE

THE PARK AND ITS
CELEBRATED LANDMARKS

BY
MIRIAM BERMAN

SALT LAKE CITY

For All My Family and Friends

First Edition
Copyright © 2001 Miriam Berman

Published by
Gibbs Smith, Publisher
P.O. Box 667
Layton, Utah 84041

Orders: (800) 748-5439
www.gibbs-smith.com

Designed by Miriam Berman
Printed and bound in Hong Kong

Library of Congress Cataloging-in-Publication Data

Berman, Miriam 1942-
        On Madison Square: the park and its celebrated landmarks
        by Miriam Berman—1st ed.
        p. cm.
Includes index
ISBN 1-58685-037-7
1. Madison Square Park (New York, N. Y.)—History. 2. New York
(N.Y.)—History. 3. New York (N. Y.)—Bibliography. 4. New York
(N.Y.)—Buildings, structures, etc. I. Title
 F128.65.M18 B46 2000
  974.7'1   00-012785

TABLE OF CONTENTS

ACKNOWLEDGEMENTS

My interest in Madison Square began almost twenty years ago, after I had maintained my design office in the Flatiron Building for some eight years. At first in the building's penthouse, with exquisite views of sunsets on the Hudson River, and then on the twelfth floor facing Broadway, with a perfectly framed aerial view of the park. It was at this second location within the Flatiron that my curiosity in the area was heightened and my interest in historic preservation was piqued. I witnessed my flawless view of the Metropolitan Life Insurance Tower slowly vanish — in the name of progress — and fill with the terraced facade of the Madison Green apartment complex. It was also about this time that I agreed to attend a postcard show with a friend. I decided that I would look for images of my office building, completely naive to the fact that the Flatiron was the most reproduced image ever applied to the picture postcard. While thumbing through collection after collection, looking for my subject, I began to see familiar images of Madison Square Park — at first views of the park looking south with the Flatiron — then views looking north, east and west. I noticed magnificent buildings in this place I had grown so familiar with that were no longer there, as well as wonderful structures that had survived.

After ten years I left the Flatiron Building for one of the most beautiful buildings on the park, between 25th and 26th Streets on Fifth Avenue. Now my view from the third floor brought me even with the treetops of Madison Square Park and my collection grew from solely postcards to books, periodicals, prints and collectibles on the area — and soon, this material began to weave a story of an exciting and vibrant place with an abundant history.

It has taken the help of many people to make this book a reality, starting with Peter Simmons, who at the time was with the Museum of the City of New York and was supportive about this project from the beginning. It was he who introduced me to Gibbs Smith, a New York City enthusiast, Utah-based publisher, photographer and artist in his own right, who immediately became enamored with the idea of producing this book.

Having evolved over such a long period of time there are a multitude of people who touched this project both physically and emotionally. To mention just a few, I will start close to home with Daniel May of the Metropolitan Life Insurance Company Archives and Jennifer Fulton of the New York Life Insurance Company Archives, both who made their vast collection of materials available to me. Nathan Willensky for sharing his unique and extensive personal archive of area memorabilia, and Jerzy Koss, the quintessential photographer of Madison Square, who has so brilliantly captured its every nook and cranny for the past thirty years. To Sharon Ullman, executive director of the Twenty-Third Street Association, who has kept me current on all the area happenings, and whose organization, which reaches from 18th Street to 28th Street and river to river, has her heart deeply planted in Madison Square.

To John Lambert of the Gramercy Brass, who enlivens the park each summer with his concert series. It was John who asked Captain Kenneth Force, director of music at the United States Merchant Marine Academy in Kings Point, New York, to create an arrangement for brass of "The Madison Square March — Two Step," by Edward J. Abram. I had found this piece of sheet music, published in 1894, many years ago. I was not only fortunate to hear John's rendition performed by his group upon the 150th anniversary of Madison Square, but also a second composition by Robert Ruggieri, a composer and Madison Square resident who recorded the piece electronically.

To Eileen Morales and Elizabeth Ellis of the Museum of the City of New York Archives for opening the doors of their collections to me and for their time and patience on this project. Also thanks to Borinquen Gallo and Mary Beth Cavanaugh of the New-York Historical Society Archives and to Madeline Kent, archivist of the Durst Collection at the Old York Library. Thanks also to Jane Crotty at Baruch College and Amy Lambach of the City Parks Foundation for all their support.

Thanks to my many friends and colleagues who shared my enthusiasm and often surprised me with unique and wonderful additions to my collection that ultimately enhanced this project.

To Melinda Hunt, who helped clarify some of the park's early history and who I came to know when she decided to commemorate the anniversary of the potter's field that occupied Madison Square in the late 1700s. The "Circle of Hope" served to brighten the park in 1994 during one of its visually bleak periods with its decorative fence enclosing a circular planting of corn, both planted and harvested by children in early summer and fall respectively.

To my very loyal assistants throughout the years — particularly Erica Ilton, Anne Swett, and for the past seven years Sophia Stavropoulos — who did not realize that woven into their design assignments would be the required reading of *Time and Again* and occasional research trips to the library, building department and various institutions to unearth some part of the history of Madison Square. To Peter Bittner and Fletcher Manley for their photographic knowledge and support.

Finally a special thank you to Madge Baird, my editor, who helped make this project so enjoyable and manageable, keeping me on track, and whose expertise served to make clear many thoughts I had imbedded in my manuscript, asking the right questions to extract those still in my head.

This wonderful painting by Gibbs Smith, showing the Flatiron Building looking north from Twenty-first Street, was created in 1985 on one of his many sales trips to New York City.

It was said that Daniel H. Burnham, the architect of the Flatiron Building, maintained an office in the cupola of the domed building seen here on the left, at 170 Fifth Avenue. Preceding the Flatiron by about three years, and designed by Robert Maynicke, it would have offered Burnham the perfect vantage point from which to keep a careful watch on the progress of his building. Today the dome is brilliantly gilded and its thirteen stories house a variety of businesses.

INTRODUCTION

By the late 1800s Madison Square boasted an ambiance often compared to that of Paris, a mix of stately homes and establishments for elegant entertainment. Here one could dine at the finest restaurants, enjoy the very best theater and stay at some of the most luxurious hotels in the city, among the most popular the Fifth Avenue Hotel and the Hoffman House. Many of these structures served as political gathering places for both the Democratic and Republican Parties, and as a home away from home for United States presidents and foreign dignitaries. To promenade through Madison Square Park in one's finest was a favorite entertainment. Elegant lifestyles contrasted sharply with those of the less fortunate, many of whom very often made the park their temporary shelter and looked to the well-to-do for an occasional handout. Both the rich and poor could be seen taking refuge on one of the many benches shaded by a variety of impressive trees planted in honor of American presidents and fallen war heroes. One could also admire statues to Admiral Farragut, William Seward, Chester Arthur and Roscoe Conkling. (Conkling actually lost his life in the park. He was felled by the Blizzard of 1888 when he suddenly found himself lost in the square on his way home from work; his statue was erected where he was found.) From the Worth Monument, just outside the park's western boundary, one could view the many impressive parades and processions that made their way down Fifth Avenue. This spot was temporarily enhanced on three separate occasions: with the erection of the Washington Centennial Arches in 1889, the Dewey Arch in 1899 and the Victory Arch in 1919.

Madison Square was an inspiration to many. O. Henry wrote several of his short stories about life in and around the park. Stanford White's first and last architectural commissions were created in and around the square. John Sloan interpreted the area in his paintings and drawings, as Stieglitz, Steichen and the unique Byron family of photographers captured it on film. Dr. Parkhurst, the colorful pastor of the Madison Square Presbyterian Church, sought to expose the scandals and corruption of life in the city and was most successful utilizing some unorthodox undercover methods. Madison Square was a place of lust and incipient lust, from the much-publicized affair of Evelyn Nesbitt and Stanford White to Saint-Gaudens's controversial sculpture of Diana atop Madison Square Garden and Bouguereau's painting *Nymphs and Satyr*, which graced the red velvet walls of the Hoffman House bar. Even the innocent voyeur who paused just a moment too long at the windiest spot in the city—at the point of Flatiron Building at 23rd Street—to admire an upturned skirt was soon shooed away by an officer assigned to his post, known as "23-Skidoo."

As the Flatiron Building approaches its centennial year, it has witnessed a myriad of significant architectural transformations. Upon its completion it joined the newly built Appellate Courthouse, which was to become a showcase for noted artists and sculptors who provided works of art for both the interior and exterior of the Palladian-style building. The Flatiron briefly overlooked the elegant Fifth Avenue Hotel, Stanford White's Madison Square Presbyterian Church, as well as his Madison Square Garden, and soon bid them all a fond farewell. Certainly its biggest loss was the demise of the Jerome Mansion, with whom it had shared the park for so many years. Home to Jenny Jerome, who grew up to become the mother of Winston Churchill, this impressive residence was replaced in 1965 by the unsympathetic Merchandise Mart. The emergence of the New York Life Insurance and Metropolitan Life Insurance Buildings on the park's east side brought a sense of stability and grandeur. The fifty-story Met Life tower had given the twenty-one-story Flatiron but a half-dozen years to command the park, but by no means did it overshadow it—nothing could take away from the Flatiron's prominence. Its freestanding position at the crossing of the two great thoroughfares of Fifth Avenue and Broadway was as unique as the famous landmark itself.

Early in the century Madison Square became a popular tourist attraction, and small auto-buses engaged visitors to the city at the Flatiron Building. It was from here that departures took place for citywide "Seeing New York" excursions. Today an endless array of public and private vehicles momentarily deposit their passengers just one block away at the Worth Monument. This small obelisk-like structure stands directly opposite the Flatiron on its very own triangular island created by the crossing of Fifth Avenue and Broadway. From General Worth's actual burial site, where he was interred in 1857 with several of his war momentos, visitors have a unique vantage point of the park as well as the famed Flatiron. Cameras snap as tourists are captured with this architectural monument. Chances are the only photo they will take home showing a New York City skyscraper from streetscape to skyscape will be that of the Flatiron, for nowhere else can one stand back far enough to so fully appreciate many of the city's architectural wonders. Madison Square affords this luxury to the Flatiron along with several other landmark buildings. Ironically one of the best views of the Empire State Building is to be had from the west side of Madison Square Park.

The Flatiron Building now stands at the newly appointed gateway to what has become known as "Silicon Alley." This is a loosely designated area filled with cyberspace businesses that starts at Madison Square and runs south along Broadway to somewhere below Houston Street. Edgar Saltus might have been mistaken when he wrote of the Flatiron in an article for *Munsey's Magazine* in 1905, "Its front is lifted to the future. On the past its back is turned." Often compared to the prow of a massive ship moving forward, the Flatiron appears today to have our future in tow.

Madison Square and the Flatiron are an inseparable duo and will always be a source of inspiration to all who come to enjoy this special place. Its delightful sense of pomp and elegance of a vital past will continue to endure for generations to come.

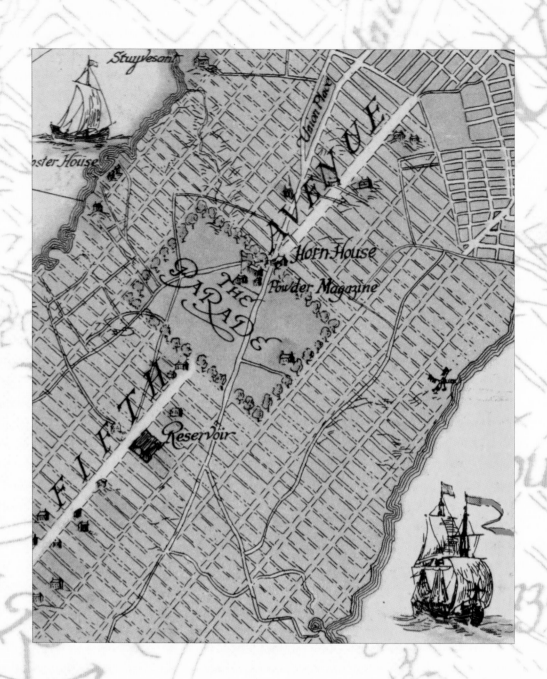

1
MADISON SQUARE PARK

THE PARADE GROUND

The area of Madison Square Park was designated a public space in the first city charter on April 27, 1686, by the Royal Governor of New York, Thomas Dongan. He was the second English governor and received 300 pounds from the citizens for his famous Charter of Liberties. This charter gave the people long-desired revenue from the Long Island Ferry as well as ownership of public markets, docks and all unappropriated lands on the island.

The middle section of Manhattan Island, sometime after its settlement, received the name Bloemendal, which translated to "a vale of flowers." Indian trails led over and across it and wild animals prowled the dense woodland. The area was described by Washington Irving as part of "a sweet rural valley, beautiful with many a bright wild flower, refreshed by many a pure streamlet, and enlivened here and there by a delectable little Dutch cottage, sheltered under some sloping hill and almost (the towering) trees." Bloomingdale Road (Broadway) was opened with the Act of June 18th, 1703, as stated in the preamble of the Act of November 25th, 1751, which provided for keeping the road in repair. In this act it is mentioned that the road was laid out the breadth of four rods from the house of John Horn at 23rd Street and ran through the Bloomingdale district to the house of Adrian Hooglandt at 116th Street. Later it was extended to 147th Street, where Bloomingdale merged with the Kingsbridge Road. The Bloomingdale Road became a local thoroughfare that led to the hamlet of Bloomingdale and was widened in 1760.

The Eastern Post Road, or Boston Road (the road to Boston), was the first highway laid out through the length of the island. Its origin was at the junction of Bloomingdale Road and what was to become 23rd Street. The character of the land was broken and rocky, diversified with swamps and a briery growth. It held slight attraction to the farmer and so only a small portion was initially inhabited by settlers prior to the city Charter of 1786.

South of the crossroads of the Old Post Road and Bloomingdale Road was a swampy piece of land of about eleven acres belonging to the city corporation. In 1745 it was presented to Sir Peter Warren as a gift. Later it was purchased by Henry Gage, who, after the revolution, returned to England, having sold the property to Isaac Varian for sixty pounds. Varian, a farmer, also owned a large tract of about fifteen acres situated on the west side of Broadway between 26th and 31st Streets, which he bought from John De Witt in 1787 for 1,280 pounds. John Watts, a lawyer and merchant, owned the property to the east of the Varian farm. Known as Rose Hill Farm and situated "out of town," the 131 acres extended from 21st to 30th Streets and from Broadway to the East River with the Post Road crossing the estate. He purchased this land as his country home, while maintaining his city home on Great Dock Street (Pearl Street). Rose Hill Farm was in the Watts family until 1786.

By 1780 the city had reacquired nearly 37 acres between the Bloomingdale and Post Roads, and by 1784 the Common Council had received petitions for leases of these Common Lands. Beginning at

OPPOSITE

1 *This unusual decorative map shows Manhattan Island oriented south to north. It graced the cover of the book* Fifth Avenue Old and New, *and depicts the Parade Ground, an immense open green within which Madison Square Park as we know it today exists. As it dwindled in size, this spacious area became the inspiration for the city to put aside an open area for the people, farther uptown, that became Central Park.*

9

26th Street, the land was divided into lots of about 5 acres and numbered, leaving Middle Road (now Fifth Avenue) between the Post and Bloomingdale Roads. The triangular piece of land created by the junction of the Post and Bloomingdale Roads was left open until 1807, when it was ceded to the U.S. government for the site of a military arsenal.

The arsenal, a well-constructed building of stone and brick enclosed by a seventeen-foot-high wall, served as one of several military posts in the city. Here military organizations during the War of 1812 carried out their drills and maneuvers and were on alert for possible British attack from the north. The arsenal was contained within a forty-four-block area (238.7 acres) bounded by 23rd and 34th Streets and Third to Seventh Avenues. This was the earliest formal delineation of Madison Square Park. Known as the Parade, the area bore the remains of a potter's field, which had been established there in 1794 as a burial ground for victims of a yellow-fever outbreak. By 1797 the potter's field was closed and moved to Washington Square.

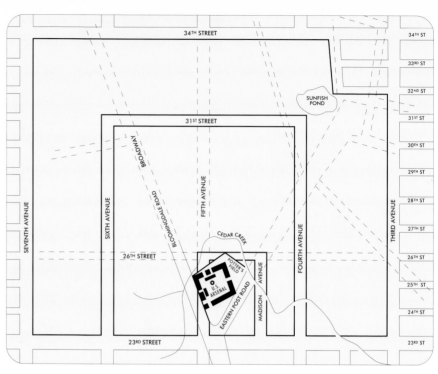

2 *This map defines Madison Square, in three phases: 1) as it was originally conceived as a Parade Ground in 1807 from 23rd to 34th Streets and Seventh to Third Avenues; 2) reduced in size to 23rd to 31st Streets and Sixth to Park Avenues in 1814; and 3) reduced once again in 1845 to its present size, 23rd to 26th Streets between Fifth and Madison Avenues.*

In 1811 the grid plan for Manhattan streets was created by New York City's Commission on Streets and Roads, which included Gouverneur Morris, Simeon De Witt, and John Rutherford, who had been appointed in 1807 by Mayor De Witt Clinton. Over a three-year period, the commissioners exhausted several ideas, among them, a "natural city" plan, one that would preserve the configuration of the land and the courses of the streams, which proved impractical, as did the square-block plan used in Philadelphia, which was also rejected. As was reported in an issue of the Metropolitan Life Insurance Company's newsletter, the *Home Office,* legend was that in 1810, on a somewhat overcast hot summer's day, this group of men found themselves pondering their problem on the banks of a stream that crossed what is now Madison Square Park. This stream (known as Cedar Creek or Madison Stream) had its origin to the west of the square, and after passing along the line of Broadway turned eastward and skirted the northern end of the park. It then passed south, where it broadened into a pond, following a southeasterly course toward the East River, into which it emptied at about 17th Street. At a spot along the stream (the corner of Madison Avenue and 23rd Street), the commissioners stopped and began to sketch out several design solutions with the tips of their canes in some freshly screened sand. When the sun suddenly came out and the rays struck the large wire screen that workmen had used to sift the sand onto the bank, the screen cast a shadow of lines that created a rectangular pattern over one of the commissioner's island sketches, suggesting the scheme of broad avenues running the length of Manhattan with cross streets placed closer together and running river to river. It is said that this chance happening led to further studies and an eventual adaptation of this "sun-shadow" street plan. Elizabeth Hawes, in her book *New York, New York,* enhances this concept by commenting that, "seen through the grid plan, the city appeared to be caught, contained and diffused behind fine netting or grating."

THE HOUSE OF REFUGE

In 1814 the Parade Ground was reduced in size to 89.1 acres, with boundaries from 23rd to 31st Streets and Sixth to Park Avenues. It was at this time that the area was named Madison Square, after James Madison, the fourth president of the United States. In 1825, well after the War of 1812, when fear of foreign invasion had passed, the arsenal became home to New York's first House of Refuge, opened by the Society for the Reformation of Youthful Delinquents.

3 *The charcoal rendering by E. P. Chrystie shows a view looking up Bloomingdale Road (Broadway) from Love Lane (22nd Street). Clearly visible is the House of Refuge, with tracks in the snow veering towards Eastern Post Road. The Buck Horn Tavern is seen at the lower right of the illustration.*

4 *This map depicts the area illustrated in the Chrystie rendering and shows Eastern Post Road cutting diagonally across what is to become Madison Square Park. The arsenal as depicted in the map in figure 2 is now the House of Refuge.*

Its first occupants were six boys and three girls. Its purpose: the care and reformation of juvenile offenders. Charles Dickens visited here upon occasion. The area was still quite rural, with a lovely cherry orchard adjacent to the arsenal site.

There were several outbuildings surrounding the House of Refuge that housed workshops and businesses. In one such structure was the factory of Stephen C. Demarest and Company, a producer of brass nails and whips. The floor above housed a chair factory owned by Captain Seaman. On June 20, 1839, a fire broke out in the center of the Demarest workshop and quickly spread to the top floor of the women's wing of the House of Refuge. An alarm was sounded and the inmates were

11

5 *The U-shaped House of Refuge evolved from a simple rectangular structure when separate wings for boys and girls were added later.*

taken to safety. Suddenly, from almost out of nowhere, ex-Alderman Bunting of the Fourth Ward appeared on horseback. He had built the arsenal and quickly took command in an attempt to salvage what he could. Moments later the fire engines and crowds of onlookers were upon the scene. Water was suctioned from the closest source of water, Sunfish Pond (fig. 2), and at the site volunteers formed a bucket brigade and were able to get the fire on the roof under control. During all this excitement, a group of roughnecks emerged from the crowd, set on destroying the cherry trees and stripping them of fruit. They were soon subdued by Justice Taylor of the upper police court and order was soon restored. The entire building was destroyed, with the exception of the women's wing, and the House of Refuge was relocated to East 23rd Street until 1854, then moved to Randall's Island. The Eastern Post Road was closed the same year as the fire.

THE OPENING OF MADISON SQUARE PARK

In 1844 James Harper of publishing fame was chosen mayor, and during his administration commissioners were appointed to acquire the lands forming the square as we know it today. In 1845 Samuel B. Ruggles, who had developed Gramercy Park, petitioned the city for the completion of Madison Square Park. The park was reduced to its present size of three city blocks, 23rd to 26th Streets between Fifth and Madison Avenues. The land was acquired by the parks department,

6-6a *The original geometric design of Madison Square Park as it appeared in 1844. The engraving shows the alignment of East 25th Street with the northerly east-west path of the park.*

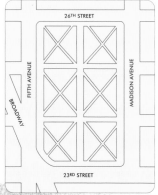

leveled, seeded, and grassed, and ordered open on May 10, 1847. A crude wooden fence was put in place, as well as paths (6,600 feet of walks) connecting the streets and avenues. A rigid diamond-like design of intersecting paths was created. A north-south path ran through the center of the park, and two other paths ran east-west in alignment with 24th and 25th Streets. The six large blocks created by these three intersecting paths contained simple crisscross footpaths. By the mid-1850s, private brownstone dwellings lined the perimeter of Madison Square. Well-to-do and prominent families took great pride in their park-side addresses.

7 *This rectangular structure by Sir Joseph Paxton, which appeared in* Gleason's Pictorial Drawing-Room Companion, 1852, *was one of the early designs for the Crystal Palace, its shape suggesting that this was the proposal for Madison Square. The final design, by the architects Charles Geldemeister and George J. B. Carstensen, was erected behind the reservoir at 42nd Street and Sixth Avenue. The massive cast-iron and glass building, about twice the size of this early plan, utilized several of Paxton's design elements, including a modified version of the immense semicircular rosette window and the decorative flanking turrets.*

THE CRYSTAL PALACE

In 1851 a committee led by Edward Riddle and his associates petitioned the city for the free and sole occupation of Madison Square Park for the purpose of erecting a building for an Industrial Exhibition of All Nations, which was to become a part of the first World's Fair. At a cost of $150,000, it was to be constructed of cast iron and vitrified translucent glass, and fashioned after the Crystal Palace of Hyde Park in London. The finished structure would be at least 600 feet long, with a width of 200 feet, all but covering the entire park. The building's proposed height of 183 feet would make it one of the most unique edifices ever erected in the world. Its purpose would be the promotion and evidence of the general prosperity of other nations. This exposition would afford the public a chance to study the productivity of other countries without traveling to distant parts of the world.

Arguments were made for how such a venture on this site would benefit the immediate neighborhood of Madison Square Park. Its location was believed to be ideal by the sponsors because of its proximity to the New York and Harlem Railroad Depot at the northeast corner of the park. Visitors would have to be fed, housed and transported, and local merchants could not help but sell more goods. The construction, as well as the removal of the building itself, would provide employment for hundreds. The terms that were drawn up in the final proposal were that the structure could only occupy the square for two years and that an iron railing with the necessary gates for entry would be installed at a cost of $6,000. This figure was doubled before the proposal's final presentation.

These gates would remain a permanent enhancement of the park, and the grounds would be restored to their original state, with every effort made not to disturb the trees. Finally, the admission charge would not exceed fifty cents.

With the publication of this proposal came much opposition, particularly from the residents of the park and those interested in preserving the integrity of the square. On the evening of December 25, 1851, concerned residents left family and friends celebrating the Christmas holiday to meet at the home of William Hurry at 3 Madison Square North, where a committee of three was appointed to prevent the signing of the proposed plan. Local residents argued that their properties on the square had been assessed and they were paying for the benefits that they derived from the square, being that of light, air and the enjoyment of this open space. Such spaces were referred to as the "lungs of the city" by the *New York Mirror*, and were believed necessary to purify and regenerate the atmosphere. They maintained that when the land was originally designated a public space, it was to benefit the health and gratification of all classes of citizens. It was argued that erecting a building for an exhibition of goods, wares, merchandise and works of art for private gain would be no more a "public building" than one for a museum or menagerie. Churches, theaters and hotels could also be considered places of public resort, but one would never consider erecting such a building in a park. The structures acceptable on such a site would have been public buildings such as a city hall or courthouse. The Crystal Palace in Hyde Park had been a national effort, not a private speculation. The Crystal Palace in this country would be small and insignificant compared with the original effort. The only good that would come of it would find its way into the pockets of the lessees of the square.

Riddle's committee concluded that if they wanted to make money, they should not interfere with the rights, convenience, health and pleasure of the public. In view of all the opposition, Riddle withdrew his application for Madison Square and requested use of Bryant Park, or Reservoir Square as it was known at the time. This, of course, was not his preferred choice, in that the massive Croton Reservoir, today the site of the main building of the New York Public Library at 42nd Street and Fifth Avenue, minimized the building's grand scale, and the surrounding shanties did little to enhance the area.

The Crystal Palace was finally erected in Reservoir Park and opened by President Franklin Pierce on July 4, 1853; it later became part of America's first World's Fair. The building was designed by George Carstenson and Charles Gildermeister. Its first president was, most appropriately, P. T. Barnum, lover of almost any extravaganza. Although the exterior was fireproof, the interior was not, and in 1858 it was almost instantly destroyed by fire.

It was only one year later, after the proposal's defeat and a couple of months before the opening of the Crystal Palace, on May 2, 1853, that Franconi's Hippodrome opened on what had been the site of the old Madison Cottage, just opposite the park, at the corner of 23rd Street and Fifth Avenue. The residents around the park could not complain about their new, rather colorful, neighbor because its location was outside the park's perimeter.

The Crystal Palace, with its many fine examples of products from foreign lands, never came to Madison Square Park. However, it is somewhat ironical that on the very site where the opposition met to oppose the plan for the Crystal Palace, the Gift Building, as it is known today, rose and was to play host annually to the International Gift Show.

BASEBALL

Before the formal opening of the park, the area had been used for various sports, among them ice skating on the frozen Cedar Creek and an early ball game called Rounders. In 1845 this English game was reportedly played here by the Knickerbocker Club, a group of sportsmen led by volunteer fireman Alexander J. Cartwright, who is credited by some with setting down the rules of baseball. In 1927 Will Irwin, in an article entitled "Highlights of Manhattan," said that it was "in this open and useless field town boys played and were introduced by a comrade, a new game. He laid out flat stones for bases, a diamond." (Although many take credit for the game's creation, it is Abner Doubleday who is recognized as its founder by the National Baseball Hall of Fame and Museum in Cooperstown, New York.)

THE WORTH MONUMENT AND TRIANGULAR PARK

With the boundaries of the park formally delineated, a large, imposing, open space to the west of the park had been created by the merging of Broadway and Fifth Avenues. In the middle of that open area, between 24th and 25th Streets, a small triangular parcel of land had been carved out by the crossing of these two major thoroughfares. Originally named Triangular Park, according to a *Valentine Manual* of 1854, it served as an extension of Madison Square Park, eventually graced with its own trees and drinking fountain.

It was upon this plot of land that a fifty-one-foot granite obelisk monument designed by James Goodwin Batterson was erected to honor Major General William Jenkins Worth in 1857. Worth was born in Hudson, New York, and served on the Niagara frontier in the War of 1812 and from 1820–28 was commandant of cadets and instructor of infantry tactics at West Point. In 1847 he was recognized for his leadership in the Mexican War: he was the first to enter the city of Mexico, and he cut down the Mexican flag that waved from the National Palace. For his efforts, Congress and the State of New York presented him with several honorary swords.

8 *Major General William Jenkins Worth.*

9 *The interment of Major General William Jenkins Worth and dedication of Worth Monument attended by national guardsmen, Masonic organizations and distinguished citizens. The monument bore bronze plaques on each side, one with a portrait of General Worth on horseback, the others inscribed with the legends "Love of Country Guides" and "Honor the Brave" and the names of the battles in which he took part.*

In 1848 he was given command of the Department of Texas, but one year later he contracted cholera and died in San Antonio. His remains were brought to New York and placed in a vault in Greenwood Cemetery. On November 25, 1857, an impressive military procession bearing his coffin carried him from City Hall to Madison Square. Thousands lined the route to see the general to his final resting place. This burial site is one of the few outside a cemetery in New York and unique in its placement in the middle of two major intersecting thoroughfares. Inside the tomb along with his remains were placed a piece of iron chain that had stretched across the Hudson River at West Point to frustrate King George's men-o-war during the revolution, a newspaper account of George Washington, copper pennies of 1787 and 1812, a medal that had been struck in commemoration of the union of the Atlantic and the Erie Canal, a Colt revolver, and copies of all New York newspapers.

It was on this very site, in the early 1900s, that the homeless gathered on winter nights to receive a chance to seek refuge from the cold. In these Bed Lines, described in O. Henry's *The Fifth Wheel,* a preacher acting as a spokesman stood on a pine box and attracted those of means to donate their change to house these unfortunates for a night. One evening he proclaimed to the passing affluent, "No man ever learned to be a drunkard on five-cent whisky." John Sloan captured a similar sight in his painting *The Coffee Line,* where unemployed men wait for coffee offered by a local newspaper.

In 1941 the Worth Monument was cleaned and, directly adjacent to the north end of the fence, a black-marble service building was erected by the Department of Water Supply to house the main valves of the Catskill Aqueduct Supply. (Today the building no longer serves that function and suggestions have been made for its removal.) The fence and the monument continued to deteriorate

10 *The Worth Monument is seen surrounded by its decorative iron railing and corner lampposts. Triangular Park, this tiny island of refuge with its own trees and drinking fountain, is captured in this lively engraving made from a painting,* A May Day in Fifth Avenue *by Wordworth Thompson in 1880.*

over the next fifty years. In October 1987, after years of neglect and vandalization, the Worth Monument was included in the Adopt-a-Monument program set up by the Municipal Arts Society. Working in conjunction with the Parks Department's Division of Art and Antiquities, the private

contractors, Historical Arts and Casting and Integrated Conservation Resources, performed specialized work on the obelisk, reliefs, base, and ornamental fence surrounding the monument. A rededication ceremony was held on November 28, 1995, with Henry J. Stern, Paul Porzelt and Thomas S. Woodruff, a descendant of Major General Worth, in attendance. Brigadier General Robert J. St. Onge, Commandant, United States Corps of Cadets, United States Military Academy; the United States Military Academy Color Guard; and Field Music Group, the "Hellcats," were among those who paid tribute to the achievements of General Worth.

11 *Steven A. Baird, of Historical Arts and Casting, of West Jordan, Utah, completes an inventory of the Worth Monument's cast-iron fence components during its restoration process in 1995. He and his company, along with Integrated Conservation Resources, of New York City, worked as private contractors in conjunction with the Parks Department's Division of Art and Antiquities performing specialized work on the obelisk, reliefs, base, and ornamental fence.*

12 *William Allen Butler.*

13 *Flora M'Flimsey in distress as illustrated by A. Hoppin for Butler's* Flora M'Flimsey of Madison Square *when the poem was published in book form by Rudd and Carleton, New York.*

WILLIAM BUTLER AND FLORA M'FLIMSEY

In 1857 prominent New York lawyer William Allen Butler, who lived nearby Madison Square at 37 East 19th Street, created the fictitious character Miss Flora M'Flimsey of Madison Square. She was born in a short piece he wrote for *Harper's Weekly* entitled "Nothing to Wear." Butler was inspired by his five sisters, who continually used the phrase "nothing to wear" in connection with their busy social calendars. Even the popular and simple everyday pastime of promenading through the park prompted a change of wardrobe. The poem asserted that no matter how many dresses one owned, if a dress had been worn more than once or lacked the correct accessories, it could not be seen again. "Nothing to Wear," seemingly inspired by wealthy New York City society, became so popular that it was picked up by a publishing firm and produced as a small volume, becoming an instant classic throughout the country and abroad and putting Madison Square on the map. Following are just a few of the poem's 305 lines:

Miss Flora M'Flimsey, of Madison Square,
Has made three separate journeys to Paris,
And her father assures me, each time she was there,
That she and her friend Mrs. Harris . . .
Spent six consecutive weeks without stopping,
In one continuous round of shopping . . .
For bonnets, mantillas, capes, collars, and shawls;
Dresses for breakfasts, and dinners and balls;
Dresses to sit in, and stand in and walk in;
Dresses to dance in, and flirt in, and talk in;
Dresses in which to do nothing at all;
Dresses for Winter, Spring, Summer and Fall—

Butler concludes the poem with a moral turn:

O ladies, dear ladies, the next sunny day
Please trundle your hoops just out of Broadway,
From its whirl and its bustle, its fashion and pride,
And the temples of Trade which tower on each side,
To the alleys and lanes, where Misfortune and Guilt
Their children have gathered, their city have built;
Where Hunger and Vice, like twin beasts of prey,
Have hunted their victims to gloom and despair . . .
Then home to your wardrobes, and say, if you dare—
Spoiled children of fashion—you've nothing to wear!

THE FORMAL DESIGN OF
IGNATZ PILAT'S MADISON SQUARE PARK

Madison Square Park took on its present look when it was designed in 1870 by Ignatz Anton Pilat and William Grant. Pilat, who was from Austria, studied botany at the University of Vienna and was employed in the Imperial Botanical Gardens of Schönbrunn. He became one of Frederick Law Olmsted's most influential assistants in the designing of Central Park. The original shape of the park had been perfectly rectangular, with a very slight rounding of the southwest corner where Broadway crosses Fifth Avenue (fig. 6). As vehicular traffic developed, the roadway towards the southwest corner of the park became very congested.

It was noted in an 1871 annual report of the Department of Parks, that Broadway at 25th Street was to be widened ". . . to provide additional and necessary carriage-way for public accommodation. . . ." This plan was carried out by starting at the easterly curb of Broadway at 23rd Street, and sweeping around with a regular curve of large radius to the line of the easterly curb of Fifth Avenue at 26th Street. This added about sixty feet to the width of the carriageway and created the irregular shape of the park as it is today. The design of Madison Square Park was characterized as Victorian informality. The elegant curved walkways around a large central lawn, with fountains thirty feet in diameter, both north and south, was an ingenious solution for a relatively small park, its circular design providing relief from the city's inflexible grid plan. There were no paths to take one directly across the park; instead, meandering and intertwining paths invited one in and gently led one around and through, giving the illusion of a park much grander in size. One would be unlikely to repeat subsequent walks in exactly the same pattern. Its seductive design slowed down the harried and gave haven to those who wished to linger and enjoy the bucolic surroundings. O. Henry, in his short story "Squaring the Circle," the plot of which concludes at Broadway and Fifth and 23rd Street, describes the rigidity of the city's design: "Nature moves in circles; Art in straight lines. . . . Nature is lost quickest in a big city. The cause is geometrical, not moral. The straight lines of its streets and architecture . . . coldly exhibit a sneering defiance of the curved line of Nature." Here in Madison Square Park, within a few feet of his account, nature was captured and enhanced within three short city blocks. This classical design remains, for the most part, intact today.

14-14a *An early wide-angle view of Madison Square c. 1895. The spider-like plan of curved paths in Ignatz Pilat's plan for Madison Square Park in 1870.*

It was thought that the drastic reduction in the size of Madison Square from the almost hundred-acre park may have inspired William Allen Bryant and Andrew Jackson Downing to adhere to their plan for a large city park. Their efforts were realized when construction commenced on Central Park ten years later.

ILLUMINATING THE PARK

In the early to mid 1800s, Madison Square was illuminated by oil and gas lamps scattered around and throughout the park. On Fifth Avenue between 23rd and 26th Streets, elaborate decorative gas lamps lit the roadways (fig. 37). It was in 1880 that the New York City Gas Commission authorized the Brush Electric Illumination Company to set up a generating station at 25th Street powering a series of arc lights that converted many of these elegant gas lamps to electric (fig. 42) along Broadway between Madison and Union Squares. By July of 1881 the Brush Company had been commissioned to install additional lighting at Madison Square Park in the form of "sun towers." At the top of a mast of 160 feet was a circular carriage, to which were attached six enormous electric lamps of 6,000 candlepower each. This carriage could be raised and lowered from a galley located eighteen feet off the ground, from which workmen could replace the carbons each day. Supposedly, these lights could be seen from the Orange Mountains fifteen to sixteen miles away. Unfortunately, they were almost blinding to people standing nearby, and the ladies complained that they appeared almost ghostly in this bright light.

Images if Madison Square in the 1880s show Fifth Avenue and Broadway filled with utility poles laden with endless lengths of electrical and telephone wiring. The notorious blizzard of 1888 brought down the many of these ice-covered wires, most of which had to be severed for safety reasons. This event motivated the city to bury most all utility wires by 1894.

15 *The Brush Electric Light Company installed additional electric lighting in Madison Square Park.*

By this time Edison was well on his way to introducing the incandescent light bulb and by the early 1900s decorative cast-iron lampposts were electrified and lit the city streets (see cover). A few are still found on Madison Square.

TRANSPORTATION

Stagecoaches and private carriages that were the major source of human conveyance in the early 1800s often stopped at Madison Cottage (fig. 39), which had opened on Madison Square in the late 1830s. At about the same time, one was able to board a rail car from the old New York and Harlem Railroad Depot (fig. 86), located at 26th Street and Madison Avenue. These horse-drawn cars would be driven up Fourth Avenue to 42nd Street, where they were directed onto rails and attached to an engine for the trip out of town.

8981. CAB-STAND AT MADISON SQUARE, NEW YORK.   COPYRIGHT, 1905, BY DETROIT PUBLISHING CO.

By the 1850s street rails had been installed along the old coach routes, and horses continued to draw cars that were designed to sit upon these rails, offering a smoother ride. By May 1865 the 23rd Street Ferry was established, linking New York City to Pavonia, New Jersey, offering an efficient connection to the Erie Railroad Line. Travelers were able to purchase their fares at the Erie Railroad ticket office located at Fifth Avenue and 23rd Street (the site of the future Flatiron Building) and easily board a westbound streetcar on 23rd Street.

The Hansom cab was invented in 1840 by an English architect named Joseph Hansom. A line of these horse-drawn vehicles could be seen parked around the edge of Madison Square awaiting a fare—five dollars for the day or one dollar per hour. With rail connections so readily accessible and all the fine hotels located to the west, visitors from out of town could procure rides here to whatever destinations they desired in the city.

Between the 1860s and 1880s, cable-car lines were installed on 23rd Street and Broadway, and by 1878 the elevated railway was running high above Sixth Avenue. The busy streets of the early 1900s around the park were a mix of various vehicles—both horse-drawn and horseless. The new addition of motorized carriages and double-decker buses created a chaotic atmosphere. With the second Madison Square Garden being home to the first auto show, the area fast became a popular backdrop for showing off new automobile models and their powerful capabilities. The first subways were installed at about this time, and soon the cable cars were eliminated and their tracks were torn up or buried.

The crossing of Broadway and Fifth Avenue at 23rd Street had always posed quite a challenge for both vehicular and pedestrian traffic. All at one time, a horse-drawn vehicle on Broadway could negotiate crossing Fifth and continue on Broadway, a vehicle on Fifth could cross Broadway and continue on Fifth, and most difficult of all, vehicles heading east or west on 23rd Street would have to pass this "long crossing" without the aid of traffic lights and islands of safety. With the introduction

16 *The Hansom cab was considered a non-sporting two-wheeler; the driver sat above and behind the cab. Some of these coaches were gaily colored with paintings on each side. Images might include a Swiss landscape, an Indian fight, a steamboat plowing through mountains of foam, or flying trotters. Many were said to have been rendered by the likes of Winslow Homer and other artists who later made names for themselves in the art world.*

of the automobile in the early 1900s, one or two mounted police assigned to this crossing at 23rd Street seemed, for the moment, to be in control of the traffic situation. By the 1920s and '30s, there was actually parking available in the middle of the two merged thoroughfares near the southwest corner of Madison Square Park (fig. 130). This was further complicated by the fact that, at the time, Broadway and Fifth were designed for two-way traffic. The short-lived traffic towers, located along the avenue throughout the city, provided lookout points from which traffic controllers could try to correct congested situations. One of these was installed at 26th Street and Fifth Avenue (fig. 80). Parking on the avenue was soon eliminated, and thanks to William P. Eno, one-way traffic was instituted. The son of Amos Eno, who built the famous Fifth Avenue Hotel (fig. 42) located at this confusing intersection, William was also responsible for the introduction of the safety island. One wonders if his interest in easing complicated traffic situations grew out of his early observations at his father's side on Madison Square.

17-18 *These two early postcard illustrations show the change in a familiar scene at the corner of 23rd Street where Fifth Avenue and Broadway cross. As the tall buildings of Madison Square North along East 26th Street begin to hover over the square, cable cars are replaced by early motorized buses.*

Today state-of-the-art traffic cones, complex painted street lines in dizzying configurations, expanded islands of safety, and traffic signals work in harmony to filter motorists through the intersecting avenues. Similar havoc occurs as Broadway slices diagonally through Manhattan and meets with other busy avenues and cross streets. O. Henry so aptly addressed this phenomenon in his short story "Mammon and the Archer," where the young hero becomes snarled in converging traffic at 34th Street, Broadway and Sixth Avenue. He describes the phenomenon as how "a twenty-six-inch maiden fills her twenty-two-inch girdle."

Real-estate agents and commercial-property owners on Madison Square throughout the years have always touted the area's convenience to all public transportation. Access to train and bus lines, if not directly on the park, has always been only a block or two away—and most have direct connections to Grand Central Station and Pennsylvania Station.

NEW YORK, MADISON SQUARE.

5TH AVE. & MADISON SQUARE, N. Y.

THE TREES OF MADISON SQUARE

In 1893 Madison Square was still a popular uptown resort. *King's Handbook of New York City,* published in 1892, said, "The Square in summer is charming with shade trees and beds of flowers. It is much frequented by prettily dressed children with their nurses, and withal is thoroughly delightful." *New York in Gaslight* painted a similar picture of the park when it said, "so bright and beautiful are the park and all its surroundings so full of life and gayety, so eloquent of wealth and splendor, is every object within view, that it is hard to realize that a little more than sixty years ago the pretty Square was used by the city as a Potter's Field. . . ."

By 1940 there were twenty-two different varieties of trees to be found in the six acres of Madison Square Park, according to the *Home Office* newsletter produced by the Metropolitan Life Insurance Company. Among them was an oriental plane tree; known for its longevity, some specimens have lived for 4,000 years. Other oriental trees from China and Japan included the paulownia, named after a Russian princess; the maidenhair, bearing nuts that the Chinese like to roast as we do almonds; and the tree of heaven, which has fernlike tropical leaves. Among other varieties of trees were the Kentucky coffee tree, Norway maple, sycamore maple, horse chestnut, catalpa, hackberry, Washington hawthorn, English hawthorn, white ash, Carolina poplar, scarlet oak, red oak, locust, American linden and European linden.

19 *The circular north garden as it appeared in the early 1900s, with the elegant Madison Square Garden Tower of Stanford White seen through the trees.*

To date, the oldest existing tree in the park is an American elm protected by its own metal railing at the park's southern end. Known as the queen of American trees and consort of the monarch, its resemblance to the English elm probably made early American settlers feel right at home. Another prominent tree, a pin oak from the Virginia estate of President James Madison, was presented by the

Fifth Avenue Association in 1936 to commemorate the centennial of the opening of Madison Avenue. Bordering Madison Avenue is a row of small oak trees planted by the Metropolitan Life Insurance and New York Life Insurance Companies, in 1920 and 1928 respectively, in memory of employees who had given their lives in World War I. On the west side of the park, near Fifth Avenue, is an oriental plane tree presented to the city in 1929 by members of the Young Australian League as an Australian tribute "to America's glorious dead."

A letter to the editor in the December 2, 1963, issue of the *New York Times* alleged that former park commissioner Newbold Morris was a "victim of a widely circulated but historically untrue legend that a dozen elms in the park line the boundaries of an old colonial road over which General Washington once passed." This theory was discounted, since the only road through the park ran diagonally from southwest to northeast (Eastern Post Road) and these elms were oriented north to south. The elms are very likely the oldest trees in the park, as the parks department places the age of these trees from 140 to 150 years, dating back to 1847, the official opening date of the park. These trees probably lined the central north-south path of the original park design.

Madison Square was home to the very first community Christmas tree, installed in the park in 1912. The very spot where this tree was placed is marked by the Star of Hope that stands at the southern end of the park's central oval lawn. This annual tradition, which was to spread across the nation, came about as a direct result of a conversation between a well-to-do Manhattanite and a visitor to the city who related to the local his feelings of loneliness without family or friends during the holiday season. A year later, through this New Yorker's generous efforts, the Adirondack Club donated a sixty-three-foot balsam tree to Madison Square Park, and New York Edison donated 6,000 feet of wire and 3,500 lights. Every night for a week the tree was lit at 5:30. On New Year's Eve, more then 10,000 people gathered in the park. A few minutes before midnight, the Edison men turned the lights off except for the star. At the stroke of midnight, a huge sign flashed out "1913," followed by another blazing "Happy New Year" in electric lights, after which all the tree lights were turned on again to burn until daybreak.

20 *Even the youngest inhabitants of nearby Madison Square showed off their finest on many a sunny day as they were paraded through the park in their ornate and luxurious prams.*

"VIEWING MADISON SQUARE . . .

. . . from the old 'flatiron' junction, the scene was Parisian, in its kaleidescopic cosmopolitan aspect. The white stone faces of the hotels that bounded the Square on the West heightened this impression. The Park at the time was thick with magnificent trees . . . well dressed visitors, dainty children and trim nursemaids occupied benches. . . . an extended line of Hansoms, four- wheelers, and coupés waited to pick up fares. . . . The street crossing at this point of the 'flatiron' was controlled by a gigantic policeman who was known and knew all the celebrities of the Square. He was the most colossal of the dandy 'Broadway Squad,' the pick of the force, all of them 6 feet and over. He wore a helmet and in his white-gloved hand a little rattan stick directed horse-drawn traffic, in the manner of a bandmaster conducting a symphony."

—by Henry Collins Brown
Fifth Avenue — Old and New, 1824–1924

THE FOUNTAINS

The 1870 park design of Ignatz Pilat included two thirty-foot circular fountains. It appears that only the fountain at the south end of the park was ever realized. Six planters and a decorative iron railing surrounded an ornate multitiered fountain.

There appeared to be a few drinking fountains located within the park. Each fountain had a common metal cup attached, from which passersby could satisfy their thirst. They were captured in one of the many Byron photos of the area at the time.

A most unusual fountain was donated to the city in 1880 by Miss Olivia Phelps Stokes, daughter of Mr. James Stokes. It was the work of W. W. Smith and stood directly in front of what today is the Met Life Building, at the corner of Madison Avenue and 23rd Street, just outside the corner of the park. The triangular fountain was built at a cost of more than six thousand dollars and stood eleven feet high. It was made of polished granite and stood on a foundation of brick. The base was of Quincy granite, and the superstructure was of white Westerly. The December 18, 1880, issue of *Harper's Weekly* described the fountain as follows:

21 *This decorative spouting fountain at the south end of the park was recorded by John Sloan in two of his paintings entitled* Throbbing Fountain, *the first painted during the day in 1907 and the second painted in 1908 on a summer night. By this time, the elaborate tiered central fountain had been removed and the water came from the center of the pool basin.*

22 *Opposite, above right: One of several drinking fountains of Madison Square captured here in a Byron photo. The small structure behind the fountain was designed by Jacob Wrey Mould, who worked with Calvert Vaux in creating many of the decorative structures within Central Park. It was originally built as a music pavilion.*

Carved radiating consoles separated the three sides from the string course, above which rise columns, the shafts being of polished porphyry. Over the tablature of these columns rise carved dolphins, reposing upon the angles of the triangular dome, and terminating with the finial. The horse troughs received water from the mouths of twin dolphins, the drinking fountain from a foliated shell.

When dismantled in 1957 by the parks department, several momentos were found in its foundation. In a lead case, besides a plaque with Miss Olivia Stokes' name, were a few water-soaked copies of the *New York Herald*, a Colton's Map of New York City, the business card of James Muir (a plumber of 29 East 18th Street), a restaurant menu offering a full-course meal for 25 cents, and a timetable of the Baltimore and Ohio Railroad, noting its thirty-six-hour service between Chicago and New York. The two bases, weighing more than three tons each, and the fountain's more than twenty sections were safely stored until they found their new home at the Sulfolk Museum at Stony Brook.

23 *Located directly across from the Metropolitan Life Insurance Building, at the corner of 23rd Street and Madison Avenue, the Olivia Phelps Stokes fountain drew its water from the old buried Cedar Creek.*

STATUES AND MONUMENTS

WILLIAM SEWARD – 1876 The first statue to be erected in the park was that of William Seward, at the southwest corner of the park at Broadway and 23rd Street. The figure represents the statesman seated in a senatorial chair of Renaissance character, one hand holding a scroll and the other a pen. The sculptor, well known for his small terra-cotta sculptures found in many New York City households, was Randolph Rogers, who maintained a studio just off the park at Broadway and 28th Street. Seward was a U. S. senator from New York before the Civil War and later became Lincoln's secretary of state. He was responsible for the purchase of Alaska.

THE ARM OF THE STATUE OF LIBERTY – 1876 The arm and head of the Statue of Liberty had been brought to the United States to be exhibited at the Philadelphia Exposition. In 1876 the statue's arm was installed in Madison Square Park, just opposite the Worth Monument at 25th Street. It was here for about six years to raise money to bring over the rest of the statue and to build its foundation on Bedloe's Island.

24 *The unveiling of the William Seward Statue. While Seward was described as a man of "all head and no legs," the statue appeared to depict him just the opposite, leading to the conclusion that the body of this Rogers statue did not belong to Seward. Apparently a casting in bronze of a figure of Abraham Lincoln signing the Emancipation Proclamation was appropriated in an effort to save metal. The head of Lincoln was removed and replaced with a casting of Seward's. Even more strange is the fact that there had been an attempt on Seward's life by an accomplice of Booth the very same night Lincoln was assassinated.*

25 *During its stay in the park, the arm of the Statue of Liberty, by Frédérick-Auguste Bartholdi, was mounted on a low stone structure. A modest entrance fee of fifty cents allowed one to proceed up into the torch and enjoy the same view that Jack Finney chose for his lovers Si and Julia in* Time and Again.

THE FARRAGUT MONUMENT – 1881 The monument of David Glasgow Farragut, which now stands at the north end of the park, was a unique collaboration between architect Stanford White and sculptor Augustus Saint-Gaudens. It is considered one of the finest examples of American art. Saint-Gaudens represented the admiral standing with his legs apart as if on the deck of his ship, with marine glasses in hand and his coat blowing in the wind. The monument was erected to honor Farragut for taking his fleet past the forts in Mobile Bay. The finished figure of bronze was eight feet five inches in height, slightly smaller then originally planned. The pedestal on which he stands was designed by Stanford White. It was executed in North River bluestone and formed a bench with a tall back within a shallow circular shape. On the back of the bench in low relief is the admiral's sword, cutting through the waves of the sea, flanked by two seated female figures, one representing Courage, the other Loyalty. In Robert Stern's *New York 1900,* the monument is described in the following manner: "The combination of realism in the statue and abstraction in the details of its base marked the Farragut Monument as a significant, if not fully synthesized, reflection of French aestheticism and American realism." White's close collaboration with Saint-Gaudens included many pieces of correspondence between the two when they were separated by work on other projects. In one exchange between them, White writes to Saint-Gaudens trying to reassure him about his concern for the size of the sculpture. He wrote in a letter dated December 27, 1879:

I tell you something which will be far worse than the Fifth Avenue Hotel. That is Bartholdi's huge hand and arm which is right opposite the Worth Monument. Here is an elevation of Madison Park from Twenty-sixth Street to Twenty-third Street. Seward would be about nineteen feet high, if he stood up. Never you mind; it is not size but guts that tells. You could stick the Parthenon inside a small ring of the Grand Central Depot.

A few months later, on February 24, 1880, he wrote again about the selection of the final position of the statue:

26 *Augustus Saint-Gaudens, sculptor of the Farragut statue and the decorative relief work of the monument base.*

27 *One of Stanford White's first commissions and his only surviving work on the park was the design of the Farragut base. He went on to contribute two other notable structures — the second Madison Square Garden and the Madison Square Presbyterian Church.*

28 *The Farragut Monument in its original location facing Fifth Avenue near the corner of 26th Street. Directly behind Farragut is Stanford White's Madison Square Garden. In a later collaboration, Saint-Gaudens topped White's Madison Square Garden, with the figure of* Diana, *which White thought was the largest base ever created for a statue.*

New York
Admiral Farragut Monument, Madison Square

I think it is a bully site and sometimes I think a better one might be found. I have gone there with lots of people, and their opinions differ as much as mine do. There has been no need of hurrying about it, as we are sure of the site, and they won't begin laying the foundations before April. I have been on the point of writing that formal application to the Park Commissioners twice, but both times have been stopped, the last time by your letter saying there should be twenty-five feet from the side-walk to the figure. This upset me, for in that site it can't be did. I went up with tape lines and found that it brought the figure just in the worst place and smack into the path.

I am very glad, nevertheless, that I was stirred up in my mind, for I have come myself to the almost decided conclusion that the 26th St. corner of Madison Park and 5th Ave. is a better place. It is more removed from the other statues and is altogether a more select, quiet and distinguished place, if it is not quite so public. It is in a sweller part of the Park, just where the aristocratic part of the Avenue begins and right opposite both Delmonico's and the Hotel Brunswick and the stream of people walking down Fifth Ave. would see it at once. It also would have a more northerly light and you wouldn't have any white reflections to dread.

Here is a larger view of the end [of the park]. Now, if it were put here, I do not exactly know whether it would be best to place him cornerwise, as in A-B, or parallel with the Avenue, as B-C. I myself prefer A-B. What do you think?

The monument was not positioned on the diagonal to the northwest entrance of the Park (A-B), but rather set back slightly into the Park facing Fifth Avenue (B-C). The Farragut Committee, Saint-Gaudens and Olmsted agreed.

In 1881, the monument was unveiled and three of the original crew of the *Hartford* were on hand. John H. Knowles and J. B. Millner drew aside the drapings, and B. S. Osborne displayed the admiral's flag to signal a seventeen-gun salute.

The advent of the automobile and increasing Fifth Avenue traffic created intolerable environmental conditions for the fragile bluestone base of the monument. In 1934 Robert Moses requested a report to determine a plan for its restoration. After careful analysis, it was decided that the base would be reproduced in matching granite provided by a quarry in Coopersburg, Pennsylvania. Large blocks of the more durable material were to be used to avoid too many joints. This proposal was submitted to Lawrence White, Stanford White's son, who approved the plan. In the spring of 1935, the granite was ordered and a work studio built on what was to be the new site of the statue, at the north end of the park. The monument would face south. Expert carvers trained at Picculi Brothers reproduced the technique of cutting bluestone in the Coopersburg black granite. All the work was executed in the park studio, and the new pedestal with the original Farrugut statue was unveiled in 1939. The old bluestone base was removed to the Augustus Saint-Gaudens Museum in Cornish, New Hampshire.

In November 1985 the Metropolitan Museum of Art assembled a major retrospective of Saint-Gaudens's work. The statue was removed from its granite base and joined the other works of the noted sculptor at the museum's exhibition. The show then traveled to the Museum of Fine Arts in

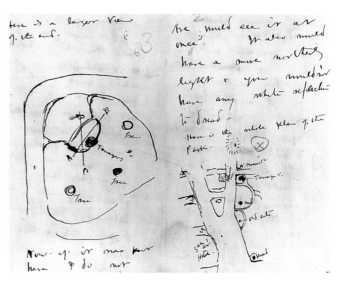

29 *An annotated page from a letter sent to Augustus Saint-Gaudens from Stanford White as they tried to decide on the best location for the monument.*

OPPOSITE

30 *George Francis Train.*

31 *Statue of Roscoe Conkling by John Quincey Adams Ward.*

32 *Chester Arthur by George Bissell.*

Boston, where it remained through May of 1986. There was an attempt by the Metropolitan Museum to permanently house the sculpture in the museum's west wing. Margot Gayle, a member of the Municipal Arts Society's Preservation Committee, along with Parks Commissioner Henry J. Stern and community leaders, had the final word, and the admiral, who had originally been created as a public monument, was returned to the park, where he would continue to stand watch as he had for more than a hundred years. This, however, was not to be his final resting place: the twenty-first century would see Farragut nudged in a slightly southwest direction to make him perfectly centered on the park's north-south axis.

ROSCOE CONKLING – 1893 From 1867 to 1881, Roscoe Conkling represented the Empire State as a Republican in the United States Senate, then he resumed his career as a lawyer. He was a most visible figure in and around the park and was often seen in full evening dress—high silk hat, white vest and necktie, and silk-lined coat over his arm—on his way to dine with his friend and fellow lawyer S. M. L. Barlow, who resided at the corner of 23rd Street and Madison Avenue. Conkling maintained a residence at the Hoffman House on Broadway, just opposite the park, a most unusual address for him since the Hoffman House was known as a haven to the Democratic Party. It was the adjacent Fifth Avenue Hotel that harbored the Republican Party, and Conkling could be seen and heard from time to time on the balcony of the Fifth Avenue Hotel speaking to his many admirers.

In the blizzard of March 12, 1888, refusing to take transportation, Conkling walked three miles from his office, located on Wall Street, to his home on Madison Square. He apparently walked through the park and stumbled into the New York Club at the corner of 25th Street and Broadway, where he collapsed. Exposure to the cold resulted, some three weeks later, in an abscess to the base of his brain. He died six weeks later in the Hoffman House. His friends erected a memorial statue designed by John Quincey Adams Ward. It is located at the southwest corner of the square. He stands as if addressing an audience.

CHESTER ARTHUR – 1898 At the northeast corner of the park is the statue of Chester A. Arthur by George Bissell. Arthur had come to New York City in 1852, where he became a lawyer specializing in civil rights cases. He became our twenty-first president after the assassination of James Garfield in 1881, and was the first president since George Washington to be sworn into office in New York City. The ceremony took place at a townhouse at 123 Lexington Avenue near 28th Street. The statue was a gift of Catherine Lorillard Wolfe, who resided on the east side of Madison Square Park.

GEORGE FRANCIS TRAIN

A living monument in the park during the late 1880s was George Francis Train. He wore a white suit that was hardly spotless and a broad-brimmed hat. He always sported a nosegay in his coat lapel, a trademark visible in an early portrait included in the book *Notable New Yorkers*. His ruddy complexion, long wavy snow-white hair, and tall frame made him easy to spot during his regular visits to the park. An eccentric who had made a great deal of his money buying property and locating towns while he was involved with the Union Pacific Railway, Train had come to establish himself as a somewhat graphic public speaker. It was said that he could be very interesting if he confined himself to one subject for more than ten seconds at a time. He had glorified the youth of America in his writings and appropriately, his Madison Square patrons were usually an attentive group of children engrossed by his rambling stories.

SKAGGARET – 1972 A modern sculpture was installed at the south end of the park between Madison Avenue and Broadway. Entitled *Skaggaret,* the piece was created by the American artist Anton Milkowski. The artist worked with Cor-Ten, a metal made by U. S. Steel that creates its own protective coating.

THE RESTORATION OF MADISON SQUARE PARK

With the exception of the major reshaping of the park in 1871, when the southwest corner of the park was sheared off to allow for a broader roadway and the Ignatz Pilat design was realized, no other major renovation was ever pursued. There were two major proposals for the park's redesign. In 1919, the year that brought the end of World War I, plans were drawn up for the Victory Arch at Madison Square, along with a preliminary plan for the reconstruction of the entire park. The design was reminiscent of the original geometric design of 1847, with a much wider center axis running north and south as well as east-west paths that would once again align with 24th and 25th Streets.

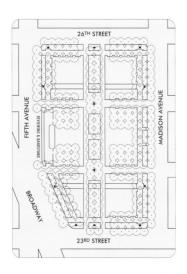

There were twenty-three monument sites designated on the plan, and elaborate tree plantings were indicated. The plan also called for a large reviewing and bandstand, and a shelter and comfort station that would have spanned 24th and 25th Streets on the west side of the park along Fifth Avenue. The master plan was never implemented; however, a temporary viewing stand was erected to complement the Victory Arch that was installed on Fifth Avenue in 1919 to celebrate the end of World War I.

A February 24, 1935, article in the *New York Herald Tribune* proposed a total redesign of Madison Square Park. The plan was to "transform the area into a formal park in the center of which will be a sunken turf panel, with a fountain at the southerly end. The upper level around the panel will be made into a promenade flanked by trees." The elms would have been "carefully preserved" and the park enhanced with two hundred new trees. The statues were to be rearranged, with the addition of a new memorial by Herman A. MacNeil of Dr. Charles Henry Parkhurst, minister of Madison Square Presbyterian Church and president of the Society for the Prevention of Crime. It was in this same article that the Farragut memorial was slated to be moved from Fifth Avenue to the north end of the park. It appears that this was the only change that was ever made at the time in the park.

In an effort to "enhance the value" of the neighborhood, a parking garage was proposed in 1963 to be built under Madison Square Park. The plan would not only have rendered the park unusable for two years but would have been a threat to the park's largest trees, some more than a hundred years old. In a letter to the editor of the *New York Times* dated August 28, 1963, Nathan Silver, assistant professor of architecture at Columbia University at the time and author of *New York Lost*, pointed to the insensitivity of Michael B. Grosso of the Fifth Avenue Association and the city's planning officials, and their "total lack of knowledge of how the city works." He went on to say, "To me a park without trees . . . would serve merely to remind me that I was a barely tolerated visitor over a busy underworld." He continued his argument by citing how these city officials were working against public transportation and the pedestrian pleasures by spending millions to draw cars to New York. Fortunately the plan for this underground project never came to be, and once again the park was saved from further destruction.

33 *This 1919 plan for the redesign of Madison Square Park would have returned it to its original 1840 plan.*

Attempts at trying to redesign, and, in some people's eyes, "enhance" the park fortunately proved futile. With its declining condition, an ambitious experimental project was undertaken in September 1979 to refurbish and maintain the park with private funds. The resources needed for the project — rake, clippers, brooms and men — were paid for by the Metropolitan Life and New York Life Insurance Companies, the Rudin Management Company and Helmsley Spear Real Estate. This, according to the *New York Times* (November 1, 1979), was the first time in New York City's history where private funds were used over a long term for the maintenance of a public park. This endeavor was planned by Donald E. Simon, a former parks department official who, at the time, was director of Urban Park Plazas. The idea was to pick a park that was in bad condition and have companies treat it as their corporate plaza. Each of the private parties in this case contributed $10,000, with the exception of the Rudin Management Company, which donated $2,500. The idea was to maintain the park by encouraging lunchtime sports like touch football or Frisbee. In other words, clean the park — not plant grass. It was felt that with the increased use of the park by more people, drug dealers would be discouraged from carrying out their business.

34 *The plan for a total redesign of the park published in the* New York Herald Tribune *in 1935.*

The road to the restoration of Madison Square Park made several detours within a thirteen-year period. It was on Friday, November 14, 1986, that ground was first broken and work commenced on what was to be the total restoration of Madison Square Park. The firm of Miceli Kulik and Associates, Inc., Landscape Architects, Site Planners and Urban Designers, were hired to restore the park in two phases: first the north end, to be followed by the southern half. Kulik chose to call this project a restoration as opposed to a renovation, like that of Union Square Park completed several years earlier. With the exception of adding two paths that were in the original park plans, squaring off the southeast corner of the park, and rotating the statue of Roscoe Conkling on its existing base to better relate to this newly created corner, his plans called for very little change in the park's 1870 layout. Kulik's original plan called for relating the Worth Monument and its small island of land as an extension of the park by means of a decorative crosswalk and additional island plantings. To keep the cost down, the inclusion of this site was not approved. The fountain at the south end of the park, part of the second phase, would be restored to its original design. Another of Kulik's hopes was to relocate the buses at the north side of the park on 26th Street. Their idling engines and constant exhaust did little to enhance the quality of the environment for those people who used the park, especially for the children who played in the newly relocated playground.

By 1988 phase one was completed. All the old asphalt paths were ripped up, and careful attention was paid so as not to disturb the trees. These paths were replaced with hexagonal asphalt blocks and edged with bluestone. All the pipe fencing within and surrounding the park was eliminated and replaced by a simple low railing enclosing the perimeter of the park and leaving the inside of the park an open space. A rather tasteful and unobtrusive children's play area was added at the northeast corner, perhaps just a little too close to the Farragut Monument. New World's Fair benches and period lampposts of the Central Park B variety were added, in addition to newly seeded lawns. A circular basin of plantings was created where once, in the original plan by Pilat, a second fountain had been planned. The cost for this first phase was $1.7 million. The second phase, which was to have begun in November 1987 at a cost of $1.37 million, never commenced. Work ceased and for almost eleven years the park became what could be described as an open-air museum. One could stroll from the beautifully restored northern end of Madison Square Park back in time to the southern end, which remained much as it had appeared at the turn of the century, except for its obvious wear and tear. Midway through the park, newly installed benches met old cement and wood benches, paths of freshly laid Belgium blocks met broken asphalt paths, and half a perimeter of elegant fencing met with broken piping that delineated the park's boundary.

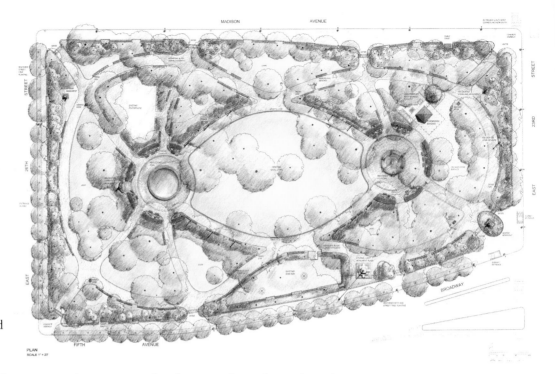

During this dormant time, efforts were made to maintain the plantings. The park was cleaned on a daily basis by uniformed workers from a newly formed group called the Madison Square Partnership, based in the Prince George Hotel. Private funds from local businesses maintained this transitional site throughout this period.

35 *This plan for the 2000 restoration of Madison Square Park shows some subtle changes but remains true to the original design. Most noticeable is the reclaiming of the southeast corner of the park.*

In October 1997 another plan for completing the restoration of the park was submitted by E. Timothy Marshall and Associates. This plan was to restore the southern end of the park, while making improvements to the original north-end restoration. The plan called for the rebuilding of the park's entire infrastructure and the improvement of the overall horticultural health of the park. This time around, the project was to have the support of the City Parks Foundation, a private non-profit organization working in partnership with the City of New York/Parks and Recreation. The City Parks Foundation organized the Campaign for the New Madison Square Park, bringing together both private and public funders for the rebuilding, restoration, improvement and, most importantly, long-term maintenance of Madison Square Park. Local businessmen, led by restaurateur Danny Meyer, Met Life chairman Robert Benmoshe and New York Life's Sy Sternberg, provided half of the $5 million and the city matched the funds. Efforts to create a BID (Business Improvement District) in the area had failed, and the city was not going to take on the project on its own. The contributors are now focused on raising an additional $6 million for maintenance and security.

What appeared to be an interim measure in achieving the park's completion occurred in 1998 as part of a city-funded capital project. The firm of Abel Bannison Butz was hired to complete the perimeter fencing by matching the already restored northerly fence, redesigning the dog run along Fifth Avenue and restoring the southerly fountain. With the completed fence in place and the new dog run now being enjoyed by the neighborhood's canines, work was again halted in early 1999. At this time it appeared as if the 1997 proposal of the Marshall firm was about to be adopted and implemented.

With the Marshall plan approved, ground was re-broken on November 15, 1999, and work commenced on the ambitious plan. The site design for the rehabilitation of Madison Square Park is a collaborative effort of HM White Site Architects, a landscape architectural and urban design firm and Patricia Cobb, Landscape Architect. Their design "reinforces the Park's formal spaces and its surrounding pastoral landscape. A hierarchy of entrances, pathways, and plazas is created through distinct design treatments. This new architectural order minimizes visual clutter and highlights the Park's unique landscape characteristics." One of the most noticeable physical changes was the "squaring off" of the southeast corner of the park, reclaiming 1,200 square feet of park space. This area had gradually diminished in size and had been utilized by motorcyclists through the years for parking. The statue of Roscoe Conkling located here was repositioned to better relate to this newly created area.

Details to match the earlier phase of the northern restoration were completed, including the installation of ornamental luminaire lampposts, World's Fair benches and hex block paths, and bluestone and granite curbs. Eight new decorative entrance gates were designed in order to close off the park at night, and remnants of the old drinking fountains were replaced with a more up-to-date design. The lawn areas were reseeded and a continuous perimeter of entrance plantings, consisting of loose flowering-shrub masses along with flowering trees and bulbs, were created to provide a transition between the city and park. An esplanade of thirty-eight new street trees bordering the park at Fifth Avenue and 26th Street completed the lush oasis of greenery.

Restoring the fountain at the park's southern end to working condition was certainly one of the most impressive additions. The recreation of the ornate central multitiered fountain, plus the six planting urns and the decorative railing that originally surrounded the large circular basin, brought with it an elegance of a bygone era. In trying to keep with the original park design, which called for a second fountain at the north end of the park, a decision was made to instead install a reflecting pool. The Farragut Monument, originally unveiled in 1881 at the park's northwest corner facing Fifth Avenue and moved in 1939 to just off center of the park's northern end, was moved slightly southwest to center exactly on the reflecting pool and was raised by a series of low steps. Plazas of bluestone were laid to encircle both the southern fountain and northern reflecting pool.

36 A rendering of the park approaching from Fifth Avenue. The Farragut Monument is seen moved slightly west, to center on the reflecting pool.

A concession stand and soft-surface picnic areas were added for the convenience of office workers who retreat to the park for their lunchtime and afternoon breaks. An abandoned underground comfort station near the southeast corner of the park houses park-maintenance storage and staff facilities.

When the restoration was completed in the spring of 2001, the full impact of the efforts to retrieve the park and return it to the original grandeur of the gilded age and Ignatz Pilat's design was realized. It has since become a haven not only for those who live and work here but for thousands who pass by and the hundreds who take refuge every day beneath its trees for a few quiet moments of reflection.

2

MADISON SQUARE WEST

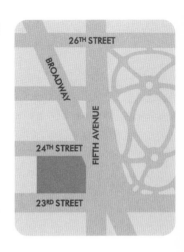

THE MILDEBERGER FARM

Madison Square West as we know it today was originally part of thirty acres belonging to Solomon Peters, a free Black. Peters, a servant to Sir Edmond Andros, the governor of New York, was granted the land, which extended from 21st Street to 26th Street between Broadway and Seventh Avenue, by Andros in 1670. He, along with other freed Blacks, had settled with their families along upper Broadway between the Bowery and Harlem. It was sixteen years later that the Dongan Charter declared the land directly east of Peters' acreage a public space. Peters' family held the land until 1716, when his widow sold it to John Horn and Cornelius Weber for the equivalent of $550. By 1736 John Horn was running a successful wagon-building and wheel-making shop on an acre of land at the junction of Love Lane (22nd Street), the Old Post Road and Bloomingdale Road. This convenient location caught the trade of wagons and coaches coming down the bumpy roads with their broken springs and loose spokes. Also located here was the Buck Horn Tavern, (fig. 3) where General George Washington and his Continental troops met citizens in 1783.

OPPOSITE

37 *A view of the west side of Madison Square showing the elegant Fifth Avenue and Broadway hotels from 23rd Street.*

38 *The Mildeberger farmhouse as it appeared along the old Bloomingdale Road (Broadway).*

Horn left his land to his son, John Horn Jr., shortly before the Revolutionary War. John Horn Jr. in turn left the land to his eight children when he died in 1815. Through the years, this land had been sold off in parts, with the exception of a parcel owned by Margaret Horn, one of the daughters of Horn Jr., and her husband Christopher Mildeberger. They maintained a farmhouse on what was becoming a growing new thoroughfare called Fifth Avenue. In 1837 the farmhouse was moved to the corner of Fifth Avenue and 23rd Street. The farmhouse and site remained in the family until 1850.

MADISON COTTAGE

The farmhouse in its new location was to become Corporal Thompson's Madison Cottage, a frequent refreshment spot for those venturing "up and out of town" on a day's outing from lower Manhattan. A notice in the *New York Herald*, May 9, 1847, read, "Madison Cottage—This beautiful place of resort opposite Madison corner of 23rd Street and Broadway, is open for the season, and Palmer's omnibuses drive to the door. It is one of the most agreeable spots for an afternoon's lounge in the suburbs of our city. Go and see."

Madison Cottage occupied an irregularly shaped plot of land. The south end of the property, at 23rd Street fronted by Fifth Avenue, was owned by the Horn family. The north end, at 24th Street fronting Broadway, had been acquired by John Treadwell and Isaac S. Hone in 1817. It was assigned to Issac's son John Hone in 1820, and he left it to his heirs in 1832. In 1851 Samuel Howland, husband of Johanna Howland, one of Hone's children, managed to acquire all the parcels of land originally owned by the Hones. This meant that between 1670 and 1857, this unique site had been in the hands of only three owners. It was John B. Monnot who bought both the Horn and Hone properties. He acquired the 40-by-203-foot Mildeberger site (Madison Cottage) in 1851 and the Howland site (the Broadway frontage to west 24th Street) in 1853.

RULES OF MADISON COTTAGE

For a guest wishing to stay the night, the rates and rules were posted:

Four pence a night for bed

•

Six pence with supper

•

No more than five to sleep in one bed

•

No boots to be worn in bed

•

Organ grinders to sleep in the wash house

•

No dogs allowed upstairs

•

No beer allowed in the kitchen

•

No razor grinders or tinkers taken in

39 *The Mildeberger farmhouse as it appeared when moved to the corner of 23rd Street and Fifth Avenue and converted into Madison Cottage. The antlers over the front entrance were transferred from the Buck Horn Tavern (fig. 3) when it was torn down in 1826 to make room for 22nd Street. To the rear, of the cottage on its expansive grounds, "cattle fairs" were held, featuring what was probably one of the first "Horse Shows" on Madison Square.*

FRANCONI'S HIPPODROME

On May 2, 1853, Franconi's Hippodrome was constructed on this newly merged site. Built by eight American showmen, including Avery Smith, Richard Sands, and Seth B. Howe, this two-story building was an open arena surrounded by a wall of brick, covered by 90,000 feet of canvas and lit by 1,000 gaslights. Its circumference of 700 feet housed a 40-foot-wide racetrack. Chariot races, circus performances and an array of exotic animals filled the arena with endless excitement. This structure, which enjoyed two years on the site, provided just a taste of what was to come some years later with the building of Madison Square Garden diagonally across the park.

40 *Franconi's Hippodrome, as pictured on the cover of a piece of sheet music titled* Hippodrome. *The composition was dedicated to the visitors to this festive spot.*

41 *Amos Eno, successful in real estate and banking, defied all odds when he opened his Fifth Avenue Hotel so "far up and out of town" at 23rd Street and Fifth Avenue.*

THE ELEGANT FIFTH AVENUE HOTEL

During the short-lived existence of the Hippodrome, ownership changed hands once more with the purchase of both parcels by Amos R. Eno. An ambitious entrepreneur, Eno had formed a partnership with John J. Phelps in 1831 in a dry goods business located on Exchange Place at the rear of the Old Merchants Exchange. They had little capital and made their purchases at auction. They experienced great success, and soon Eno's interests turned to real estate, where he made his fortunes. He was founder of the Second National Bank and later the Garfield National Bank.

In 1858 Eno announced his plans to build what was to become the elegant Fifth Avenue Hotel. His critics named his venture "Eno's Folly" because it was thought to be too far up and out of town. He moved his family to a house on East 23rd Street just slightly off of Madison Square Park in order to keep a watchful eye on his new undertaking.

Eno soon proved all skeptics wrong, and under his close supervision the hotel opened its doors in 1859. The white marble building, designed by Griffith Thomas and Son, rose six stories, could accommodate eight hundred guests, and was said to have had the first passenger elevator. The hotel had one hundred suites, each including a parlor, bedroom with fireplace, dressing room and bathroom. Four hundred servants tended to the visitors and fifty coaches awaited guests to take them to their respective destinations. Beautifully decorated public rooms on the ground floor were late-afternoon meeting spots for gold speculators and Wall Street brokers. Here discussion was usually about the closing rate of gold and the Erie Railroad. Financial bulletins posted on walls were constantly scanned to determine the way the market would react the next day. Upstairs, men weary of talking business found themselves in brightly lit parlors where they could flirt and chat with elaborately attired women looking their fairest. They were known to tell these fashionable charmers everything but the truth.

The hotel was opened under the management of Colonel Paran Stevens, but it was his wife who was credited with making it such a success. It was said of Mrs. Stevens in *Harper's Weekly* of April 13, 1895, that she was a woman of "great courage, great energy, and great force . . . very tough, very game, very able, very entertaining, exceedingly interesting . . . impulsively generous and kind." One way in which Mrs. Stevens turned Eno's Folly into Eno's success was by instituting a fourth meal, or "late supper." This meal was available to guests for an additional $2.50 a day. Dinner would be served in the hotel's ornate dining room where seating was arranged at long tables to accommo-

42 *The Fifth Avenue Hotel as it appeared in an early photo ca. 1880. This image clearly illustrates the building's unique shape as it fronts both Fifth Avenue and Broadway between 23rd and 24th Streets.*

date twenty to thirty guests at a time. Here they had the opportunity to become better acquainted with one another and, after dining, could withdraw to one of the second-floor parlors to further socialize. They had the option to return to the dining room if they wished for an additional "late supper." Friends of guests, who might have joined them for the social hour, incurred no charge for this meal.

Mrs. Stevens' other marketing strategies were just as revolutionary. From the time that Fifth Avenue first began cutting its way up Manhattan Island, a little before the Civil War, having a residence on Fifth Avenue was regarded as "quite equivalent to a title." By the late 1800s, Fifth Avenue, from Washington Square up to 42nd Street, was a strictly residential stretch of brownstone fronts. Mrs. Stevens was the first to allow shops on this holy site, with several commercial shops located on the street level of the Fifth Avenue Hotel. Mrs. Stevens' efforts to encourage commercial development on Fifth Avenue were regarded as sacrilege by those who resided on the avenue. When tobacco merchant Peter Lorillard objected, Mrs. Stevens replied, "You would not mind now, would you, if it were a tobacco shop?" Knox Hats and Maillard Chocolates were two Fifth Avenue Hotel shops that achieved great renown. Knox became known for giving new hats to visiting statesmen in return for their old ones. One such exchange was the hat of Abraham Lincoln. Lincoln also favored chocolates from Maillard, and they were frequently served at the White House during his term. These candies were considered to be the "Opulence of the Metropolis in Gifts." Originating in Montalimar, France, prior to 1840, Henry Maillard brought his confectionery business to New York City in 1848. After fire destroyed his chocolate factory at 619 Broadway, he relocated at 116 East 25th Street and established his retail shop on the first floor of the Fifth Avenue Hotel. In this wonderfully ornate shop, under a richly decorated ceiling of an allegorical representation of *Fame* by Charles Mueller, one could enjoy the very best chocolate ice cream and admire a myriad of confectionery delights.

43 *Businessmen and hotel guests crowd the Fifth Avenue Hotel lobby as they discuss the affairs of the day. Many sport high hats, some perhaps purchased at the Knox hat shop pictured to the left of the building's main entrance in figure 42.*

44a *An advertising card for Maillard chocolates.*

44b *The interior of Maillard, located at the hotel's 24th Street corner. Especially popular on Valentine's Day for young suitors of means was the $500 box of chocolates containing one special morsel embedded with a diamond ring.*

The Second National Bank was located on the ground floor of the hotel's southeast corner, at Fifth Avenue and 23rd Street, the very spot where the business and social life of the metropolis came together. The bank was organized in 1863. Its first president was Henry A. Hurlburt, and Amos Eno was on the board of directors. This institution represented not only uptown business and investment wealth but downtown banking interests as well. It also was a pioneer in servicing the needs of both the wealthy residential citizen and the commercial population located within the Madison Square area. In 1869 Joseph S. Case, one of its tellers, observing that women were potential bank customers, provided a special windowed parlor with desks for tellers and bookkeepers, where women could take care of their transactions. This feature became popular with emerging bank institutions. In the basement directly beneath the bank were the offices of the Fifth Avenue Safe-Deposit Company, which housed vaults containing 2,500 safes and compartments for use by local patrons and hotel guests.

45 *A reception for General Grant was held on November 20, 1865, at the close of the Civil War. Held in one of the parlor rooms of the Fifth Avenue Hotel, the general greeted guests and afterwards sat down to a banquet in his honor with his wife and invited guests.*

The Fifth Avenue Hotel was a resplendent success. Governors, senators, ambassadors, generals and admirals were all received at its doors. Every United States president from Buchanan to McKinley made the hotel his home while visiting the city. Several great orators held court from the balcony directly above its entrance, President Lincoln being among the most memorable. General Grant always occupied rooms 43 and 44 on the 24th Street side during his visits. Many royal visitors, including Don Pedro (the last emperor of Brazil), the Crown Prince of Siam and Prince Napoleon were welcomed. The most famous of these visitors was the Prince of Wales. From Bowling Green to the Fifth Avenue Hotel, 300,000 spectators lined Broadway to greet the prince upon his arrival. As the son of Queen Victoria, this first royal visitor to the United States stirred unparalleled public interest and excitement. The Fifth Avenue Hotel became a focal point, with scores of onlookers trying to get a glimpse of the handsome young prince. His visit was credited with the immediate success of the hotel. It was considered quite a coup for the Fifth Avenue Hotel, believed to have been so remotely located.

POLITICS, FIRE AND THE AMEN CORNER

On April 12, 1861, the Civil War broke out. The hotel became the meeting ground of "the forces that were organized to preserve the union" and was not only a refuge for politicians but was "the headquarters of all the gigantic forces, passions, and animosities aroused by this 'fratricidal' war." It was also the gathering place for New York's movers and shakers. Among them were Jay Gould and Jim Fisk, controllers of the Erie Railroad and creators of Black Friday, the financial panic that occurred when the two tried to organize a corner on the gold market. There were "Larry" Jerome of equestrian fame, shipping magnate Cornelius Vanderbilt, and "Boss" Tweed, known for his schemes of graft and fraud. The hotel's eclectic atmosphere also made it a haven for many notables in the arts, including Mark Twain, Edwin Booth, and Stanford White. Twain was once mistaken for a newsboy when another hotel guest, spotting him carrying his habitual armload of daily newspapers, requested a paper and offered him payment. Twain promptly obliged and gave the proper change. Thomas Nast, the well-known political cartoonist, had the honor of ordering the first drink at the Fifth Avenue's well-appointed "new bar" in 1882, as depicted in his cartoon "Caught in the Act." By the 1870s the hotel found itself surrounded by fine shops, restaurants, casinos and theaters where the well-to-do could find a multitude of diversions to suit their every social whim.

A tragic fire took place at the Fifth Avenue Hotel on December 10, 1872, snuffing out the lives of twenty-two hotel employees. The fire had started about 11:15 P.M., December 9, and by midnight the entire 23rd Street side was ablaze. It was believed to have started in either the stairwell or elevator leading to the laundry on the top floor. Most of the guests were in bed when the fire broke out, but being aroused by the commotion of firemen dragging hoses through the corridors and up the stairs, panic broke out and they wasted no time gathering their belongings and racing downstairs. When the fire was contained, a room-by-room search was conducted. A fireman, entering a 12-by-12-foot room located directly under the roof, a dormitory for the maids and laundry women, found bodies piled at the room's only window, which had been fitted with bars. The victims, unable to force the windows open, were slowly asphyxiated. Just two years prior, this attic room had been inspected by the New York superintendent of buildings and pronounced safe. Besides the great loss of life, damage was estimated at between $75,000 and $100,000. Edith Wharton makes reference to this event in one of her short stories, "New Year's Day." The Fifth Avenue Hotel, a fire, and an apartment on 23rd Street opposite the hotel figure significantly in this tale. Wharton, as a child, lived directly across from the Fifth Avenue Hotel, at 14 West 23rd Street, and would have been about ten years of age at the time of the tragic event.

THE SIDEWALK CLOCK

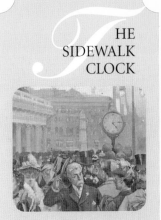

A fashionable throng is seen in front of the Fifth Avenue Hotel with its famous sidewalk clock in the background. It was made of cast iron and built by the Helca Iron Works in the 1880s.

The clock's movement is by Seth Thomas, the oldest clock maker in America.

NYC
LANDMARK
THE SIDEWALK CLOCK
AT 200 FIFTH AVENUE

AUGUST 25
1981

46a *Images of a bygone era reveal that the sidewalk clock in front of the Fifth Avenue Hotel was a favorite meeting spot.*

46b *The clock continues to inform the hurried crowds of the 21st century the correct time of day.*

47 *The famous "amen corner," located in the lobby of the Fifth Avenue Hotel, in session.*

Looking North of Twenty-third St., New York City.

Just two years prior to the fire, in 1870, a hotel guest witnessed from his fifth-floor window a gentleman rising from bed to start his day. It was Nathan Benjamin, a wealthy businessman who lived next door to the Wharton residence at 12 West 23rd Street. A few moments later the guest heard a commotion outside the brownstone. Benjamin had been brutally murdered in his home. The mysterious crime with a host of suspects, including the victim's son, was never solved.

A famous Fifth Avenue Hotel institution for over twenty-five years was the "amen corner." Notable Republicans would meet in the lobby and start a discussion. As the subject grew more intense, the group would repair to a bench in the main corridor and continue the debate. Instituted by Thomas Collier Platt, the Republican boss of New York State, it was here where many decisions that helped shape American and world history were initiated. Boss Platt made sure that the issues raised were given the proper attention, whether in Albany or Washington. The plan to make Ulysses S. Grant president was conceived here. In 1876 another gathering inspired by William C. Whitney contested the election of Samuel J. Tilden, who had received 51 percent of the popular vote, and demanded an electoral vote recount, thereby giving the presidency to Republican Rutherford B. Hayes. Here in 1884 Dr. Samuel Dickenson Burchard gave his famous "Rum, Romanism and Rebellion" speech against the Democrats. Theodore Roosevelt cultivated a couple of his political moves here. In 1886 he became a candidate for mayor of New York against Abram S. Hewitt and Henry George. Roosevelt set up his headquarters at the hotel and became known, because of his love of the West, as the "cowboy candidate." He lost the election to Hewitt, coming in third. In 1898 he once again found himself at the Fifth Avenue Hotel, when members of the Republican Party met in the "amen corner" and placed his name into nomination for governor of New York. He was elected governor and in 1900 became McKinley's vice-presidential candidate; in 1901 he became president upon McKinley's assasination.

A FOND FAREWELL TO THE FIFTH AVENUE HOTEL

With Madison Square becoming a more commercial center and more fashionable hotels opening farther uptown, the Fifth Avenue Hotel closed its doors in 1908. Seven thousand dollars passed over

48 *The Fifth Avenue Building is home today to the toy industry. However, it is also from here that the 23rd Street Association carves out a small space from which to oversee the well-being of Madison Square and its environs.*

A FINAL TRIBUTE TO A GRAND HOTEL

Hundreds of loyal club women from Brooklyn and New York who had periodically assembled for meetings at the old hotel, where they were invariably treated with the utmost respect and consideration, paid the owners the following tribute:

With every stone from out thy walls,
Some cherished gem of memory falls,
And some sweet voice, long silent, calls.

Adown thy halls of red and white,
Shine faces fair, with eyes alight,
Long vanished into yester-night.

Was ever inn so loved before!
"Home" seemed large writ above thy door,
And glad was he who paid the score.

Good-by, old tavern! On thy site,
May rise some pile made rich and bright
With marble and with Malachite.

But thousands still shall pass the spot,
And with dim eyes, where thou art not,
See thy gray ghost there, unforgot.

—Kate Upson Clark, July 30, 1908

the popular Fifth Avenue Hotel bar on its final day, when thousands of devoted patrons flocked there to buy their last drinks and purchase bottles of their favorite liquors.

The Fifth Avenue Hotel was replaced in 1909 by the Fifth Avenue Building. Owned by Eno's son, William P. Eno, he insisted that the new structure, designed by the architectural firm of Maynicke and Franke, retain certain characteristics of his father's resplendent hotel. The new multistoried building kept the hotel's basic shape, with its broad marble corridors following the original building plan. A banquet hall and the Oak Room bar, located off the main lobby, utilized wood paneling from the old hotel, evoking to this day the elegance of a bygone era. At its inception, the Fifth Avenue Building housed almost exclusively the menswear industry. The toy companies who solely inhabit this structure today were for the most part not in existence at the time, with most of the toy industry then centered in Germany. It wasn't until the outbreak of World War I that the toy business really began to develop in the United States, and around that time the first toy companies moved into the building. The industry remained strong, even though a great deal of it shifted back to Germany between the wars. By the end of World War II, the toy business was well established in the United States and most toy companies settled in the Madison Square area. By 1964 the expanding toy industry was overtaking the building and pushing out the menswear tenants. It was at this time that the building management, taking note of the industry's steady growth, decided to renew only the leases of toy and toy-related businesses. The International Toy Center, as it is known today, is the largest permanent display of toys and Christmas decorations in the world. Each year more than 20,000 buyers and 1,500 manufacturers from all over the world descend on the center in February for the International Toy Fair. The sale of the building in 1950 marked the first time in a hundred years that the property passed from the hands of the Eno family.

MADISON SQUARE THEATER

The Madison Square Theater, located adjacent to the Fifth Avenue Hotel on West 24th Street and erected by Amos Eno, was leased in 1879 to Steele MacKaye, one of the most gifted men in show business and theater design. It was formerly the site

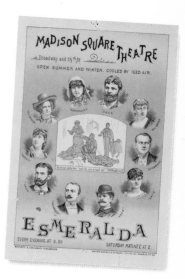

49 *A Madison Square Theater program from the summer season of 1882, with images of the cast of characters of one of its successful runs,* Esmeralda. *One of the theater's up-to-date features was its cooling system, explained in the program: "Cooled in summer by pure air passing over tons of ice."*

50 *Madison Square Theater was immediately adjacent to the Fifth Avenue Hotel on West 24th Street.*

of Brougham's Lyceum Theater, Fifth Avenue's first theater, which housed the Daly Company. The interior of the Madison Square Theater was wrought by a collaboration of some of the best-known artists, artisans and inventors of the day. It was described by one critic as the most exquisite theater in the world. Thomas Edison worked with MacKaye, advising him on the installation of the first electric footlights. Louis Comfort Tiffany and Candace Wheeler were two of several partners in a decorative arts firm known as the Associated Artists, formed in 1879. Wheeler was known for her decorative needlework and her promotion of profitable industries for women, which led to the formation of the Society of Decorative Arts. Tiffany and Wheeler worked together to create a lavishly embroidered curtain for the theater. She used a process that she patented called "needle-woven tapestry," a technique that produced scenes of great richness and depth.

51 *This illustration was featured on the cover of a* Scientific American *magazine depicting the newly installed double stage of the Madison Square Theater.*

52 *The interior of the Madison Square Theater, showing the elaborate curtain created by Louis Comfort Tiffany and Candace Wheeler. Clearly visible high above the stage is the proscenium arch that housed the production's musicians.*

Madison Square Theater was the first to introduce the backstage double-decker elevator to speed the changing of sets. Now there would be only a two-minute wait between scenes, a vast improvement for the staging and fluidity of performances. This unique feature was demonstrated to the audiences after each play. Another of the theater's extraordinary features was the positioning of the orchestra in a balcony above the stage, at the top of a proscenium arch.

Hughson Hawley, a scenery painter, was brought over from London to render backdrops for the new theater. He had caught the attention of Thomas Wisedell, one of the architects of the theater, who suggested that he might try his hand at architectural rendering. He rented his own studio and was soon accepting commissions. This led to an astounding career in which he produced over 11,000 commissions, including impressive renderings of the Metropolitan Life Tower and the Flatiron Building.

The theater's opening-night performance of *Hazel Kirke* on February 4, 1880, proved a great success, running for six hundred nights. Hawley was credited as the scenic artist for this production. Other popular productions included *Jim, The Penmen; Captain Swift;* and *Trip to Chinatown,* all by Charles Hoyt, the George M. Cohan of his time; and *The Professor,* written, produced by and starring William H. Gillette.

THE ALBEMARLE HOTEL AND THE HOFFMAN HOUSE

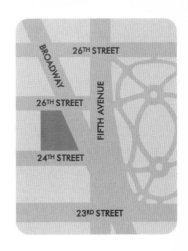

At the corner of 24th Street and Broadway stood the Albemarle Hotel, built in 1870. It shared the block between 24th and 25th Streets with the Hoffman House. The ground floor of the Albemarle was occupied by the House of Budd, one of the city's largest men's haberdashers. In the late 1860s Samuel Budd's successful business had originally been located directly across the street, on the ground floor of the Fifth Avenue Hotel. It soon outgrew this shop and moved to more spacious quarters in the new Albemarle, where it remained until 1913. This unique shop catered to an exclusive clientele that included U. S. presidents and prestigious clients such as statesmen, lawyers, doctors and many famous actors. The store was run with a rather informal flair and served as an occasional spot for a social rendezvous. Located in what was the heart of the theater district, it would not be unusual to find a performance taking place in the back of this grand emporium, with members of the makeshift audience taking their seats upon the counters. The Albemarle Hotel held onto its name, even after it was bought out by the Hoffman House Company.

In 1845, at the southwest corner of 25th Street and Broadway, Ferdinand Schaetler, a renowned German cabinetmaker, occupied a one-story building and its surrounding grounds. He was brought to this country from Hamburg by a congressional committee that was assigned to find a craftsman competent to make a model of the facade and Corinthian columns for the Capitol Building in Washington. Schaetler was very successful at his craft, and his work can be found in both Trinity and Grace Churches, as well as St. Patrick's Cathedral. His rent was $800 a year, a considerable amount to pay at that time. In 1860 John T. Hoffman, who served as mayor of New York City from 1866–68 and as governor of New York from 1869–71 offered Schaetler a ninety-nine-year lease and increased his rent to $1,000 a year. Considering this far too much, Schaetler decided to move and the site was cleared to make room for the Hoffman House. In 1877 the Reverend Eugene A. Hoffman, dean of the Theological Seminary of the Protestant Episcopal Church of Chelsea Square, commissioned John Butler Snook to design the Hoffman House. This luxury hotel was to occupy the corner site on Broadway at 25th Street, just opposite the Worth Monument, until 1915.

53 *An engraving showing the Albemarle Hotel, directly behind the Worth Monument obelisk and the Hoffman House, the two adjoining structures to the right.*

54 *The Reverend Eugene A. Hoffman.*

45

NYMPHS AND SATYR AND THE HOFFMAN HOUSE BAR

It was "considered the utmost in New York life to be seen at the Hoffman House," according to a well-known lithograph that advertised a cigar named for the hotel. In one such poster James J. Corbett, Lillian Russell, John L. Sullivan and Amos Rusie stand outside the hotel as passing carriages make their way up and down the avenue. "Charley" Noonan ran the cigar counter for many years and amassed a fortune from his earnings. One of the main attractions at the Hoffman House was its noted bar, one of the most famous of any in this country. Here, for the price of just one drink, you could eat the equivalent of a full-course dinner, created from an assortment of dishes on the free-lunch counter. You were expected, however, to tip the waiter a quarter. It did such a phenomenal business that it became known as the $1,000-a-day bar. Upon its walls hung the highly controversial painting that dominated this room—*Nymphs and Satyr,* by Adophe-William Bouguereau. *Nymphs and Satyr* was first shown at the 1873 Salon show and received mixed reactions. The French critic Ludovic Baschet claimed that the artist "had depicted a rather risky subject with charm and delicacy." Legend had it that after one consumed a succession of drinks at the famous bar, it appeared as if "the nymphs stirred and rearranged their veils and garlands."

The first owner of this notorious painting was John Wolfe, a leading New York art collector. He had re-created a room in his private residence reminiscent of a European museum in which to house the work of art. Edward Stokes, one of the owners of the Hoffman House, acquired the painting in 1882 at a sale of Wolfe's paintings. It was to spend the next twenty years hanging beneath a red velvet canopy, lit by a crystal chandelier and reflected in a large mirror over the bar in the Hoffman House. Its association with Stokes gained it even more notoriety, in that Stokes had spent four years in Sing Sing for shooting Jim Fisk, his rival in a love triangle with Josie Mansfield.

Nymphs and Satyr became synonymous with the Hoffman House and so popular an image that reproductions of it were to be found on labels inside cigar boxes, on silver matchbox covers, on plates, urns and even bathroom tiles. It was at the Hoffman House that Robert Sterling Clark, a young Yale graduate, first saw this painting that made a lasting impression upon him. When Stokes died in 1901, the painting was sold to a gentleman whose family thought the subject an embarrassment, and it was placed in storage for over twenty-five years. By chance, Clark had encountered the painting some years earlier, in 1934, and directed his close friend, Herbert Elfers of the prestigious Durand-Ruel Galleries, to the owners. Elfers purchased the painting and in turn sold it to Clark in June of 1942. When it was shown the following year at Elfers'

JOHN B. SNOOK

One of the most noted architects of his time, John B. Snook had a successful career spanning almost half a century. Born in 1815, Snook was brought to New York from London and began an apprenticeship in building at the age of twelve. He studied architecture under Joseph Trench, and in 1846 they designed the Stewart Department Store located at 10th Street and Broadway. Trench soon moved west, and Snook took over his practice.

In 1872 Snook designed the first Grand Central Station at 42nd Street, thus rendering the old railroad depot on Madison Square obsolete and available for what was to become the first Madison Square Garden. Two years later in 1879, after the success of the Hoffman House, Snook was asked by William Henry Vanderbilt to design twin houses for himself and his daughters on the west side of Fifth Avenue between 51st and 52nd Streets. Snook was to build two more buildings on Madison Square, a residential brownstone in the 1880s and the Cross Chambers in 1901, both at 210 Fifth Avenue.

Gallery, the art critic Frank Crowninshield, in an article for *Vogue*, expressed its reemergence as the "launching of the Nymphs once again as a symbol both of the Gay Nineties and of the happy and joyous spirit of the Second Empire." Clark eventually installed the painting in his New York apartment, and in 1959 unveiled *Nymphs and Satyr* in a ground-floor gallery in his museum, the Sterling and Francine Clark Art Institute, in Williamstown, Massachusetts.

The Hoffman House also displayed other works of art. Among these pieces were *Narcissus* by Correggio; *Holy Mother* by Demonceaux; *Russian Mail Carrier* by Chelmonski; *Boudoir and Eastern Princess* by Etienne; Ball's statue of *Eve,* in marble; and *Pan and Bacchante* by Schlessinger. Ladies were admitted to the gallery area only during certain hours of the day.

At the rear of the Hoffman House was the gambling house of Charley Reed, once the largest and best known of these establishments. Fleishman's, a ground-floor flower shop, was located at the hotel's 25th Street corner. Described by Idell

Zeisloft in *The New Metropolis*, "... it's graceful window frames showing a living picture of artistic floral decorations and tasteful groupings of ferns and palms, its wonderful footman so splendidly arrayed, and its not less picturesque delivery wagon ..." A penthouse restaurant provided elegant dining overlooking the treetops of Madison Square.

One notable and frequent guest of the Hoffman House was Sarah Bernhardt. She made her home here while performing in many nearby Broadway theaters. Percy C. Byron had been the photographer for stills for one of her plays, *Izeyl*. She was so impressed with his results that she permitted

OPPOSITE
55 *John Butler Snook*

56 *The famous Hoffman House bar, showing the installation of the painting* Nymphs and Satyr.

57 *The notorious* Nymphs and Satyr *by Adophe-William Bouguereau.*

47

Byron up to her hotel suite to photograph her for an article in *Munsey's* magazine. As was reported, " . . . she fell into each pose easily, never changing a line of her gown or allowing the photographer to make a suggestion. Everything must be perfectly natural, just as she was, without any studying out of effects." Another distinguished tenant was Grover Cleveland, who lived at the Hoffman House when he was elected president for the second time.

TOY CENTER NORTH

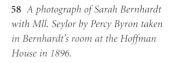

In 1908 the old Hoffman House was rebuilt at a cost of $1.3 million, making the Albemarle-Hoffman complex one of the most modern facilities of its kind in the city. Just seven years later, on March 15, 1915, the hotel closed its doors, falling victim to the development of more-fashionable hotels uptown. This left the Madison Square Hotel, directly across the park on Madison Avenue, between 25th and 26th Streets, the only surviving hotel on the square. The Kinney Estate, which also had paid more than $4.5 million for the Albemarle-Hoffman, received only $1.7 million at the time of the sale. They had, however, seen great profits while these properties were in their prime. The Broadway and Twenty-Fourth Street Company, which purchased the site, erected a sixteen-story office building on the property. It is seen under construction in figure 64. The architects for the new structure were H. Craig Severance and William Van Alen. Some fifteen years later, Van Alen designed the prestigious Chrysler Building.

58 *A photograph of Sarah Bernhardt with Mll. Seylor by Percy Byron taken in Bernhardt's room at the Hoffman House in 1896.*

59 *The remodeled Hoffman House.*

60 *The Toy Center complex.*

In 1968 a footbridge high above West 24th Street joined the ninth floors of 200 Fifth Avenue and 200 Fifth Avenue North, allowing these two buildings to function as one enormous venue for the annual Toy Fair. Because of its unique location and its business relationship to 200 Fifth Avenue, the building bears two addresses, 200 Fifth Avenue North and 1107 Broadway.

At the southwest corner of Broadway and 25th Street, adjacent to Toy Center North, is a small office building at 1115 Broadway that, like its neighbors, is home to a number of merchandise showrooms and the Toy Manufacturers of America. The TMA was established in 1916 to represent the U.S. producers and importers of toys and holiday decorations. Today the organization promotes industry growth globally and is an advocate for product safety and supporters of the proper use of advertising guidelines for children.

On Fifth Avenue and Broadway

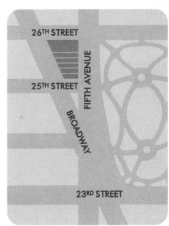

As Fifth Avenue and Broadway go their separate ways at 25th Street, these two thoroughfares form a uniquely shaped trapezoidal block, bounded on the north by 26th Street. In the mid-1850s, a row of residential brownstones lined both Fifth Avenue and Broadway. By the late 1800s several of these residences on Fifth were being altered to accommodate street- and parlor-level shops. As the area further developed commercially, it became a much-sought-after location for businesses. Its high visibility, with frontages on both Broadway and Fifth Avenue, was recognized as early as the 1870s, when Delmonico's chose their new site at 26th Street, giving their restaurant three means of access. On Fifth Avenue, brownstones were soon replaced by low commercial structures. These block-through buildings had the benefit of having "mirrored" entrances—that is, all the facades on Fifth Avenue were duplicated on Broadway. When the Lincoln Savings Bank occupied 208 Fifth Avenue and added a portico and sidewalk clock, they repeated the exact facade treatment on Broadway, including the clock. The minimal height of these buildings afforded the west side of Broadway continued exposure to Madison Square Park, especially advantageous to the Townsend and the St. James, the first two high-rise office buildings in the area, which celebrated their 100th anniversaries on Madison Square in 1996. Their dramatic presence, towering over the brownstone row on Fifth Avenue and over the park, was an early prelude to the lofty structures that would soon appear to the north and east of the park.

61 *Looking north from the Flatiron Building's short trapezoidal block between 25th and 26th Streets, whose buildings front both Fifth Avenue and Broadway.*

From Diamonds, Silver and Haute Couture to Erector Sets and Christmas Trees

Located directly behind the Worth Monument, at number 1 West 25th Street, was a small hotel named the Worth House. By the 1880s it was occupied by the New York Club. This particular site, because it was all breadth and no depth, proved to be impractical. Several different tenants tried to adapt to its awkward space. In 1887 the Madison Square Bank took over the building for its offices, with upper floors occupied by *Cosmopolitan* magazine. By the turn of the century, signage on the building indicated that it was home to, among others, the Berlitz School of Languages and the banking offices of Henry Clews and Company.

62 *A view of Fifth Avenue from 25th to 26th Streets. From left to right: no. 202, the banking offices of Henry Clews; no. 204, Knox Hats; no. 206, the jewelers, Black Starr; no. 208, the Meriden-Britannia Company and the Lincoln Savings Bank (note their sidewalk clock); no. 210, Mark Cross leather goods; no. 212, Café Martin, Delmonico's successor.*

In 1918 a new building replaced the brownstone structure, adding an additional floor. The most popular and innovative business that was to occupy this site was the Gilbert Hall of Science, so named by its founder, A. C. Gilbert, a rather flamboyant P. T. Barnum–like figure, and the inventor of the Erector Set. He took over the entire building in 1941, modernized the facade and installed six circular windows along the 25th Street entrance in which to show off his elaborate building sets and American Flyer train layouts. This street-level showroom became a favorite haunt for children of all ages. It was Gilbert who, during World War I, was credited as "the man who saved Christmas." According to an account of his life by Bruce Watson in the May 1999 issue of *Smithsonian* magazine, Gilbert found himself in Washington, D.C., in the office of the secretary of the navy. They were there to discuss toys and the nation's wartime priorities. The questions at hand were, "Should parents be asked to support America's war effort by buying Liberty bonds instead of toys that Christmas, or should the Council of National Defense impose a ban on toy purchases? Beyond that, were toys vital for the nation's morale?"

Gilbert responded by saying, "The greatest influences in the life of a boy are his toys." To demonstrate his point, he unwrapped a selection of his building toys. Before long, the people gathered for the meeting were on their hands and knees, assembling various bridges and structures. Three hours later, the council decided against the ban on toys. Gilbert's Hall of Science remained at this site on Madison Square until the 1960s, when his company was bought out by Gabriel Toys. Faint outlines of the covered portholes remained visible until the early 1990s, when Commodore and Criterion, a Christmas-decoration showroom, took over the entire building, covering the ground-floor facade with white-and-gray marble—not a pleasing choice with the existing limestone walls.

63 *A visit to the Gilbert Hall of Science, home of the Erector Set and American Flyer model trains, was on the wish list of most every child during the 1940s and '50s.*

The 200 Block of Fifth Avenue saw numerous businesses establish residency. In the early 1900s Knox Hatters occupied the ground floor of a brownstone structure at number 204 Fifth Avenue, adjacent to the Clews Banking concern. Knox, having enjoyed a longtime residency at the Fifth Avenue Hotel, continued to do business here until the brownstone was replaced by a new bank building. Housed within a rather unusual facade, a large arched window spanned almost the entire width of the building. Number 206, also a brownstone, became home to Black Starr, noted for its fine jewelry and diamonds. Although its original brownstone facade was refaced in an effort to modernize the building, it remains the oldest structure on the park's west side. In 1894, at number 208, the New York showroom of the Meriden-Britannia Company built for themselves one of the first commercial multistoried buildings on this side of the park. Roger Brothers Silversmiths had merged with Meriden-Britannia, making it the largest silver and silverplate manufacturer in the country. Upon occupying its place on Madison Square, Meriden-Britannia took great pride in its new location and issued a wonderful small brochure containing the park's history. The company's roots were to be deeply planted here, for it eventually became part of International Silver, which, to this day, maintains a showroom on Madison Square North. In the early 1900s Meriden-Brittania moved to a more spacious showroom at the northwest corner of 26th Street, with Lincoln Savings, yet another banking institution, taking its place.

The House of Redfern, a London-based women's tailoring establishment, occupied the parlor floor of an early J. B. Snook brownstone at 210 Fifth Avenue. Displayed in each of its two parlor windows, and the only hint that this might be more than a residential dwelling, were simple one-word typographical panels, one reading "Cowes," the other "London." Redfern's, with branches in Chicago and Paris, was founded in London in 1841 by John Redfern. He started his career very modestly as a draper in Cowes, a popular yachting center on the Isle of Wight, and eventually dressed the rich and fashionable who turned out for the island's Race Week. He soon earned his reputation as court dressmaker to Queen Victoria and Queen Alexandra. Redfern became a favorite designer with New York society, and his fashions eventually graced the covers of *Harper's Bazaar* during the 1880s, with commentary predicting the fabrics and colors for the forthcoming seasons. To complete her outfit, the Redfern patron need only have descended to the ground floor of 210, to the Chanut glove shop. Gloves were a fashion must and were worn at all times, except while dining—unless one's hands were unfit to be seen. In 1916 Redfern's, displaying a flair for the practical side of fashion, designed the first women's uniform for the International Red Cross.

In 1901 Snook replaced his brownstone structure with a lovely building called the Cross Chambers, created in the Belle Epoque style (fig. 69). Built for Mark Cross, the noted leather-goods company, their shop was to occupy the first two floors. The additional ten floors, designed as residential apartments, afforded its tenants elegant living and wonderful views of Madison Square Park. Mark Cross was owned by Gerald Murphy, who had inherited the business from his father, Patrick Murphy. The business had originated in Boston, Massachusetts, and not in London, as one would have been led to believe by the incorporation of the word *London* into their popular logo (fig. 61). This came about only because Murphy had many English business connections, and perhaps he also liked the idea of keeping some of the impressive Redfern clientele.

This string of small businesses, although not officially included in the Ladies Mile Historic District designation, certainly served as part of the nearby shopping environment.

64 *According to this early advertisement, Redfern's offered not only haute couture but riding habits and mantles. Mark Cross, which succeeded Redfern's at 210 Fifth Avenue in 1901, also catered to the horsey set.*

DELMONICO'S

Completing the block at 212 Fifth Avenue stood a rather large structure that was used for assembly balls and other social gatherings. It was home to the Dodworth Studios, a noted dancing school. It was here in 1870 that Theodore Roosevelt took his formal dancing classes. Mabel Osgood Wright reminisced in her book, *My New York,* about dancing lessons she took in the early 1870s with a little boy named Theodore Roosevelt, or, as he was called, "Teddy Spectacles." In a reply to a note written to him by Ms. Wright in 1903, T. R. responded, "I am much amused to think that I should have met you at Dodworth's in the old days. Even now I remember how dreadfully I danced!"

The size of the structure and the building's unique location attracted Delmonico's to this site in 1876, the same year in which the torch of the Statue of Liberty was installed in Madison Square Park. At the time, Delmonico's was possibly the most famous restaurant in the United States. It was founded in 1827 by John and Peter Delmonico in a small house on Williams Street. It had several locations in the Wall Street area before moving to the corner of 14th Street and Fifth Avenue in 1860, and eventually to its 26th Street location, where it remained for twenty years. The Fifth Avenue frontage was sixty-five feet wide and included a miniature lawn with decorative rail for outdoor dining. The main dining room overlooked Fifth Avenue and the trees, flower beds, and, by 1881, the Admiral Farragut Monument. The Broadway frontage was a men's cafe. On the 26th Street facade was the building's main entrance, leading to the upstairs ballrooms, dining rooms and upper floors.

The interior of the restaurant was lined with mirrors, furnished in mahogany, and lit by silver chandeliers under a frescoed ceiling. In the center was a fountain bordered by flowers. The floor of the cafe was ash inlaid with marquetry. Located on the second floor were four dining rooms, one each done in hues of blue, crimson, olive and drab. Sharing this floor on the Broadway side was a ballroom some fifty feet square, finished in regal red and gold, with adjacent supper and retiring rooms. Additional dining rooms were located on the third floor, along with a banquet hall that could be divided into three separate spaces if desired. The fourth floor was given over to quarters for a few confirmed bachelors. Finally, the top floor housed the servants, storage rooms and laundry.

Ward McAllister, known as the czar of New York's social empire, was responsible for selecting "the four hundred" socialites to attend the opening of Delmonico's. He believed that there were only four hundred people at any given event in New York City who knew how to behave in a ballroom.

Delmonico's was to become "the place" for social and charitable functions. Young ladies attended various social events and cotillions there, making their debuts at events such as the Patriarch's Ball. Delmonico's was host to the notable and not-so-notable, and Charles Delmonico was very much in charge of his restaurant. The Delmonicos were Swiss and adhered to strict rules of ethics. They maintained a blacklist of people not welcome at their establishment. Since the restaurant was a public facility, if an unwanted customer entered and ordered a drink from a waiter, the waiter took the order and then walked away, never to return. The embarrassed customer would soon leave on his own.

Charles Ranhofer was the chef between 1879 and 1899. It was said, "Tell him the number of your guests and nothing more, and you will have perfection." In the December 1896 issue of

DELMONICO'S —THE OPENING

On opening day, September 11, 1876, by cocktail hour Delmonico's was packed with patrons. As noted in the *Herald:*

The tide of promenaders of a bright afternoon . . . keeps right along Broadway or up the Avenue. Go whichever way they will, they now find Delmonico's doors standing invitingly open—on the Avenue as well as on Broadway. A more central location could not have been selected. . . . Here the great, formal, pompous dinner parties of the associations of the rich, the political dinners, which were only disguises for speechmaking; the happy and cozy family reunions; the tender gastronomical tête a têtes of a pair of hungry lovers just come from a feast of grand opera; and the quiet jolly suppers of convivial friends—all these will find here another gay and bright center, another happy hunting ground.

Metropolitan magazine, Ranhofer, speaking of his rich patrons, wrote, "The man of wealth who does not know how to feel the delight of giving a good dinner to his friends fails to appreciate the blessings of his fortune and no man who desires to possess perfect health and long life should be without a devoted physician and a wise cook." The restaurant also served as a meeting ground for politicians, businessmen, theater people, sportsmen, and members of the Union, Knickerbocker, Calumet and Manhattan Clubs. In November 1897 Theodore Roosevelt was once again to

DELMONICO'S
—THE CLOSING

At a luncheon in April 1899, small cards were scattered on tables announcing that Delmonico's 26th Street establishment would close its doors on the eighteenth of the month. Not a chair was vacant on its final evening. "Handshakes and nods of recognition were exchanged, and here and there tables were pulled together for groups of six or eight who had known 'Del's' for a lifetime." When midnight arrived and the crowds reluctantly departed, it was not without either a salt shaker, matchbox holder or some keepsake. One last patron getting up to leave said, "It seems like saying good-bye to home. . . . It was the saddest day in the lives of the Delmonicos when they decided to give up this lovely corner—flooded by sunshine from the park in the day, surrounded by theaters and clubs by night."

65 *Ladies lunch at Delmonico's at 26th Street and Fifth Avenue.*

66 *Residential brownstones lined Fifth Avenue between 25th and 26th Streets in this early photo showing Delmonico's in the 1880s. Redfern's, an English tailoring shop, is discreetly in residence in the brownstone directly adjacent to the famous dining establishment. The Croisic Hotel is seen on the corner across West 26th Street.*

find himself at 26th and Fifth, not as a young lad learning to dance, but as assistant secretary of the navy, addressing a dinner of the Society of Naval Architects and Maritime Engineers. Madison Square Garden and Delmonico's occupied opposite corners of the park and

67 *A promotional fan, one of the many promotional items produced by Café Martin.*

68 *The old Delmonico interior, refurbished for Café Martin with ornately decorated mirrored walls and balcony.*

69 *The old Delmonico's building with an additional floor, remodeled for Café Martin. Immediately adjacent is the Cross Chambers.*

OPPOSITE

70 *Pictured here are numbers 202 to 212 Fifth Avenue as they appeared about 1915. All the buildings, with the exception of number 202, are the same today as they appear here.*

complemented each other during their stay. For instance, during the Horse Show at the Garden, the most popular of all its events, Delmonico's offered its Horse Show dinner, which included such stable pleasantries as "bay oysters," "purée à la rein, saddle of two-year-old with horseradish sauce," and "bridle cakes with roan sauce" topped off with a "pony of brandy."

In 1899 Delmonico's, following the uptown movement of the great hotels and businesses, moved to Fifth Avenue and 44th Street, where it remained until May 21, 1923 when it closed its doors forever. The *Herald* proclaimed, "There can never be just such another place as this Delmonico's was."

CAFÉ MARTIN

On May 4, 1901, John B. Martin leased the building Delmonico's had vacated for his second restaurant, Café Martin. He raised the roof of the existing

12176. CAFE MARTIN (OLD DELMONICO'S) NEW YORK.   COPYRIGHT, 1905, BY DETROIT PUBLISHING CO.

Delmonico's structure and added an outdoor cafe. For its twenty-one-year residency, the interior of Café Martin maintained the grand tradition of elegance that Delmonico's had established. It was fashioned with comfortable banquettes and marble-topped tables, and ladies were served liquor only if accompanied by gentlemen. The foyer was most hospitable to well-groomed ladies, and it was said that masculine solitude was easily solved here. To lure prospective customers, Café Martin produced outstanding promotional materials, including colorful menus, fans and postcards — all with striking graphics. The postcards, a series, featured patrons hurriedly on their way to the corner of Fifth and 26th Street using most every means of transportation, from race cars to motorcycles to airborne vehicles. A milestone marker appeared in every scene, indicating the number of miles left to Café Martin.

It was at Café Martin, on the ill-fated evening of June 25, 1906, that Stanford White was to have his last meal on his way to the theater, prior to his demise on the roof garden of Madison Square Garden.

Today this site is occupied by the tallest structure on the block, catering to mainly high-tech and publishing firms. From 1994–99 the television studios of Fox FX occupied the first six floors. A popular morning show used Madison Square Park as a stage set, from which they broadcast several lively segments. They also held weekly sidewalk concerts in front of the building, featuring high-profile music groups.

[Map showing:]
Stevens House/Victoria Hotel ▼
◄ Ritzmann's
► The Coisic
▼ The St. James
The Serbian
Orthodox
Cathedral ►
of St. Sava
◄ The Holdout
▲ TheTownsend
Eden Musée
▼
The Western Union Building ▲

EARLY HOTELS AND A PHOTOGRAPHER TO THE FAMOUS

One frequent patron of Delmonico's, and included among New York's elite "Four Hundred," was a Frenchman by the name of Richard de Logerot, Marquis of Croisic. He and his wealthy American wife could often be seen eating for hours at their favorite Fifth Avenue window. He had been the landlord of the Hotel de Logerot at 18th Street and Fifth Avenue. In 1887, inspired by Delmonico's success, the couple built an apartment house called The Croisic (fig. 66) at the northwest corner of 26th Street and Fifth Avenue. A very grand hotel was later built on this site in 1911, complete with ballroom and winding marble staircases connecting the floors. The building was never used as a hotel but became an office building soon after its completion. It is said that Ethel Barrymore was the building's only residential tenant. The only vestige of the building's bygone era is to be found in the lobby, where a surviving section of the elaborate marble stairwell still leads to the second floor. Ornate architectural detailing covers the upper floors of the building, with working gargoyles that act as downspouts.

The Croisic shared the block with three brownstone structures and the Stevens' House, an early apartment hotel built in 1872 that ran the entire block between Fifth and Broadway on 27th Street. It was designed by Richard Morris Hunt for Mr. and Mrs. Paran Stevens, managers of the Fifth Avenue Hotel, and featured architectural details that one would find on some of the more elaborate hotels of the time, such as an ornate mansard roof with various-sized dormers and multiple chimneys. There were eighteen suites, each featuring a parlor, dining room, kitchen, butler's pantry and up to five bedrooms, dressing rooms and bathrooms, with servants' quarters in the attic. Several shops and a restaurant were located on the ground floor.

Apartment hotels such as the Stevens' House offered the domestic features of an apartment house, eliminating, if one wished, the kitchen in favor of a communal kitchen that would prepare meals, made to order, or provide cuisine from the house restaurant. It replaced the concierge with a manager and offered the luxuries of a hotel without the stigma of risqué living. Prospective tenants were lured by the provision of many modern amenities, including artificial refrigeration and long-distance telephones. These were commercial conveniences not available in private dwellings at this time.

By 1879 the Stevens' House was remodeled and became the Victoria Hotel, catering to the tourist trade. The photo studio of Charles L. Ritzman was located on the ground-floor level of the Victoria. Known for photographing theatrical celebrities and visiting dignitaries, his photographic galleries catered to those who collected the very popular carte-de-visite and cabinet-size photos. Ritzman's window displays on Fifth Avenue were a veritable who's who of international fame. In 1902, as the Flatiron Building began to emerge from its triangular site, his studio recorded many impressive phases of the building's construction.

THE EDEN MUSÉE

Built in 1883 in the French Renaissance style, the Eden Musée stood for thirty years at 55 West 23rd Street. It housed an extensive collection of distinguished personalities, all rendered in wax. Large groupings included twenty-two figures of rulers from around the world, another, sixteen army and navy heroes. There was also a Chamber of Horror and "Ajeeb," an automated chess player. In addition, the Winter Garden provided daily concerts and magicians. Specialty entertainers and Japanese acrobatic troupes entertained the crowds. It was the first to showcase regular presentations of films. The Eden Musée lobby, shown above, featured a life-size figure of Officer Kane, standing guard at the ticket window. His beat was at nearby Fifth Avenue and 23rd Street.

71 *The Eden Musée lobby as pictured in one of their programs.*

THE TOWNSEND AND THE ST. JAMES

The Townsend Building at 1123 Broadway and the St. James Building at 1133 Broadway, which were both built in 1896, were the earliest skyscraper office buildings to loom over Madison Square. By the 1850s the short block between 25th and 26th Streets on the west side of Broadway included a small hostelry owned by the Townsend family at the corner of 25th, two five-story brownstones and the elegant St. James Hotel at the corner of 26th. By the 1890s the Townsends decided to replace their small hotel with an office building, their intention being to include the property of the two adjoining brownstones. The owners of the brownstone directly next to their property agreed, but not Edward T. King, owner of the brownstone immediately adjacent to the St. James Hotel. The Townsends proceeded with their plans without using King's property, and the architect

72 *This photograph shows the Townsend and St. James Buildings, two of the first office buildings in the area, and how they dwarfed the low buildings directly across the street on the east side of Broadway. In the foreground is a bit of the Fifth Avenue Hotel, the Albemarle and Hoffman House. Bleachers are erected at the Worth Monument for an impending parade.*

Cyrus Eidlitz designed a twelve-story structure in a neo-Renaissance style with a limestone exterior. That same year the St. James Hotel was purchased by Joseph and Abraham Pennock. Their intention was to build another office building on the same block of equal stature to the Townsend. They, too, tried to include the King property and failed. They hired Bruce Price to create a sixteen-story building in the Beaux-Arts style in a striking combination of stone, brick, terra-cotta, iron and copper. Price's design philosophy was to create buildings that other artists and architects would appreciate; therefore, it was no surprise that the building was soon filled with architects, engineers, artists and artisans. Because the St. James and the Townsend stood along Broadway's Great White Way, they also attracted tenants from various theatrical businesses. Upon the completion of the Townsend, Eidlitz moved his architectural firm into the building. It was here that he drafted his plans for the Times Tower at 42nd Street. Almost a century later the Townsend continues to draw design-oriented tenants.

These two towering giants sandwiched the King holdout until 1908, when the Pittsburgh Life and Trust Company finally persuaded the King family to sell. The brownstone was immediately torn down and replaced by a one-story structure that was to become home to the Carl H. Schultz mineral water shop. Schultz was a pioneer in the manufacturing of artificially flavored waters. Here at The Sign of the Siphon, one could sample a variety of waters in long-stemmed glasses, dispensed

73 *This is an illustration of the actual sign that hung outside Schultz's mineral water shop. The converted "holdout," between the Townsend and the St. James Buildings, was one of many such watering spots scattered throughout the city. These waters were believed to have medicinal benefits.*

74 *The Western Union Building.*

THE WESTERN UNION BUILDING

NYC
HISTORIC DESIGNATION

THE WESTERN UNION BUILDING
AT 23RD STREET AND FIFTH AVENUE
INCLUDED IN
THE LADIES MILE HISTORIC DISTRICT

MAY 2 1989

The Western Union Building stands opposite 200 Fifth Avenue on the southwest corner of 23rd Street and Fifth Avenue. It was built as their "uptown" branch in 1883. From this location, messages were transmitted to the downtown main office by means of an underground pneumatic tube that ran 2½ miles down Broadway. The redbrick facade is in the Queen Anne style and was designed by Henry J. Hardenbergh, who maintained his architectural firm on the upper floors of the building. The 23rd Street facade rises seven stories and is topped by ornamented windows, above which run a row of pedimented dormers. This detail was highly unusual for an office building, having usually been reserved for residential structures. He would soon apply it to one of his most notable design projects, the Dakota.

from porcelain fountains topped by Tiffany lamps. On the opposite side of the shop, a wood-paneled bar served ice cream sodas and egg creams. Tables filled the back of this rather elegant watering spot. These soda shops were very popular at this time throughout the city.

As fate would have it, this tiny piece of real estate that kept the two buildings apart for nearly a century would play a pivotal role in bringing the Townsend and St. James together. At the time of the buildings' restorations in the 1980s, it was decided to link the two structures together. Not as obvious as the other "bridges of Madison Square," (located high above 24th Street, the Met Life Bridge on the east side and the Toy Center Bridge on the west side), the Townsend and St. James passageway is set back above the one-story holdout and connects the second floor of the two buildings. Unnoticed from the street, the joining of these two buildings allows them to function as one, sharing the many services offered by the management.

The ground floors of both the Townsend and the St. James have been home to various businesses throughout the years, but none so handsome as the tobacco shop designed by Stanford White in 1904 for the Havana Tobacco Company. Located in the street-level shop of the St. James, at the corner of 26th and Broadway, White created a palace-like environment of marble and tropical fantasy. The trompe l'oeil ceiling depicted an aquamarine sky as viewed through a vine-covered lattice. The room was graced by warm carpets recessed into the marble floors, a large tapestry, and murals of Cuban scenes by Willard Metcalf. The shop served the posh clientele that frequented the neighboring restaurants such as Delmonico's (26th Street between 5th and Broadway) and patrons of the nearby Hoffman House and Fifth Avenue Hotel.

The most gratifying part of the buildings' restorations was uncovering so many hidden treasures, such as the wonderful mural and elaborate rosette vaulted ceiling that graced the archway of the St. James lobby—uncovered when the dropped ceiling was removed—and the beautiful mosaic tile-work floors of both the Townsend and St. James. The mural depicts Minerva, the Roman goddess of wisdom, war and peace, with two vestal virgins. Price commissioned the mural, which was originally attributed to Arthur Brounet because it bears his signature. However, art historian William Laurel Harris, after researching the work, theorized that the mural was not a Brounet but that of the American Impressionist Willard Metcalf, who had probably collaborated with Brounet as was common practice in architectural mural painting at the time. Brounet maintained his studio in the St. James building for forty years, until his death in 1941.

The stairway of the Townsend was restored to its original beauty with the refurbishing of the cast-iron columns that support the impressive staircase. Cleaning revealed their ornately designed surfaces. All the mosaic-covered landings were brought back to life almost one square at a time. A resident design firm could not help but be curious about a logo design intricately rendered in mosaic on the floor of their offices. Several years after occupying the space, they received a design job for the New York subway system. While doing some basic research, they discovered that the entwined AETC initials in the Townsend mosaics represented the American Encaustic Tile Company, previous tenants of that space. This had been the firm that executed most of the city's decorative mosaic subway tiling.

3

MADISON SQUARE NORTH

AT THE TOP OF THE PARK

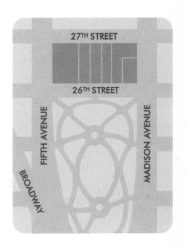

By the 1860s, brownstone-front rowhouses lined three sides of Madison Square Park, with hotels and theaters to the west. The seemingly endless row of Italianate-style dwellings along 26th Street between Fifth and Madison Avenues contrasted sharply with the variety of dwellings on the park's east side (fig. 110). Individual lot values made up a large portion of the cost of these homes, and with rising real estate values and increased interest in fashionable areas such as Madison Square, builders found it necessary to create narrower houses. To make up for the lost width, they built taller structures, that, when adjoined, made for an impressive streetscape, as on Madison Square North. These homes consisted of the basement, used for the service quarters, kitchen, and butler's pantry; the parlor floor, which included the reception room, parlor, drawing room, and dining room; and the third and fourth floors, reserved for the bedrooms and bathrooms. Owners, with their diverse needs, managed to adjust to the verticality of these homes, but not without the help of a personal staff consisting of, at the very least, a cook, a chambermaid, a nanny, a butler and possibly a coachman, whose quarters were located in the attic. Some of the earlier homes maintained stables at the rear of their houses while others rented space nearby. The rigidity of the brownstone spawned a need for inhabitants to express themselves, very often by means of their personal possessions. It was within these common walls that individuals created displays, often gaudy, filling their parlors with their worldly acquisitions of carpets, gilt-trimmed mirrors, elaborate chandeliers and overstuffed furniture.

Among the prominent residents of Madison Square North were Dr. John F. Gray, a leading representative of homeopathic medicine in Manhattan, who resided at the corner of Fifth Avenue and 26th Street. It was his neighbor, William Hurry at 3 East 26th Street, who had opened the doors to his house to concerned park residents to organize the protest against the erection of the Crystal Palace in Madison Square. Proceeding east were the homes of Frank Work and William and John O'Brian, all successful Wall Street bankers. Work, an avid coaching fan, maintained a luxurious stable at the rear of his house and, until nearly ninety years of age, drove his team of trotters up the avenue and through Central Park, many times in the company of his good friend William H. Vanderbilt. Other residents included James Burden, who had made his fortune in iron and steel, and the Schieffelin family of the noted drug house, W. H. Schieffelin and Company, who were the first to refine petroleum in New York City.

At number 21 stood the home of Benjamin H. Field, an incorporator of the American Museum of Natural History, and in 1886 the president of the New-York Historical Society. He was also prominently active in the Society for the Prevention of Cruelty to Children, which, curiously enough, was an outgrowth of the American Society for the Prevention of Cruelty to Animals.

At number 23 resided the Iselin family, who had a long connection with New York society. The imposing corner mansion had a two-story carriage house adjacent to it on Madison Avenue. Adrian Iselin was a member of the well-known banking firm of A. Iselin and Company at 36 Wall

OPPOSITE

75 *Cobblestoned East 26th Street between Fifth and Madison Avenues, showing the continuous row of brownstone homes opposite the north end of Madison Square Park. Their unified appearance was just an illusion of a row of homes conceived and built at one time. In reality, they were built over a period of time by different builders, one, two, or maybe three at a time and often not directly next to each other. To create a sense of uniformity, builders aligned cornices and windows with those of the earliest-built homes in the line.*

Street, which held interests in the Buffalo, Rochester and Pittsburgh Railway and the Southern Railway Company. He was also one of the original investors in his neighboring Madison Square Garden and, like Benjamin Field, had been associated with the American Museum of Natural History as one of its founders.

Although he did not live on the park, Herman Melville was frequently observed walking his granddaughter through the square. He was also able to keep a watchful eye on *Diana* high atop the tower of the Old Madison Square Garden from his nearby house at 104 East 26th Street, just east of Park Avenue. It was here, where he resided from 1863–91, that he wrote *Billy Budd,* among other works.

THE BRUNSWICK HOTEL AND THE COACHING CLUB

In 1871 the Brunswick Hotel opened its doors at the corner of 26th Street and Fifth Avenue on the former site of the home of Dr. Gray (fig. 148). Early hotels, with their transient clientele seeking a meal and a night's lodging, were not considered a very appealing environment for the fashionable and wealthy who wished to live here. By this time the Fifth Avenue Hotel, the Albemarle and the Hoffman House had all proven themselves "respectably residential." These imposing structures, however, were separated from the park by the wide expanse of Fifth Avenue and Broadway, while the Brunswick abutted its immediate brownstone neighbors. Soon, making

76 The original Brunswick Hotel was an early effort credited to the then-unknown Henry Hobson Richardson. He was to have a major influence on Stanford White, who was apprenticed to Richardson and went on to make so many impressive contributions in and around Madison Square Park.

a positive reputation for itself by attracting a refined British and European clientele, the Brunswick gained favor, coexisting harmoniously with park residents, who from time to time were known to utilize its dining and social facilities as extensions of their homes. This kind of successful blending, like that of the Brunswick within its residential community, eventually led to an address at a posh hotel becoming as socially acceptable as a private house. Long-term hotel residencies became popular and helped in the development and acceptability of apartment living. In *New York, New York,* Elizabeth Hawes writes, "The private accommodations of the New York hotels redefined transient living. They offered the settings of stately homes, rather than extemporized lodging, and the services attendant to such homes, magnified into public facilities."

By the late 1870s, the Brunswick expanded eastward, incorporating the Hurry residence. Its very British atmosphere and cuisine of bird and game dinners and rare-vintage wines were exactly catered to the tastes of the "horsey" set. At times it rivaled its neighbor, Delmonico's. Mitchell and Kinzler were the proprietors, and it was under their management that it became one of New York's most popular and fashionable hotel establishments. The Brunswick contained six public rooms in which guests could be served the most elaborate dinners and tempting breakfasts and lunches. Their grandest restaurant was on the ground floor, facing Fifth Avenue and 26th Street. It was patronized by the hotel guests and also open to the public. A beautiful fountain filled the center space, surrounded by a brilliant border of luxuriant ferns and hothouse plants. In the immense bay windows overlooking the park on 26th Street were vases containing almost every variety of graceful plant capable of being cultivated in the temperate zone. A ladies' restaurant also faced the park on 26th Street, and a ladies' breakfast room was located on the parlor floor at the corner of 27th Street and Fifth Avenue. In the spring of 1876, the Jardin D'ete was opened as a summer dining garden on the terrace in the court of the Brunswick. The grounds were filled with plants and flowers, and in a shady recess, a rustic arbor covered with ivy was used for small dining parties. The newspaper *The Daily Graphic* cited this new addition to the Brunswick as having the finest French food and went on to say that "the French are the best gastronomists in the world. They study the art of good living, and their *maitres d'hôtel* can surpass anybody in the preparation of a bill of fare."

The Brunswick served as the headquarters for the Coaching Club, founded by Colonel William Jay, Leonard Jerome and Colonel Delancey A. Kane, who were great enthusiasts of the sport of four-in-hand driving. It was from here that they began their annual spring and autumn run up to New Rochelle. The first public parade was held in the spring of 1876, featuring both four-in-hands and tandems led by the club's president, Colonel Jay, in a forest green suit with brass buttons, and the guard sounding his horn in the rear seat. Its unusual route went up Fifth Avenue, through Central

77 *The Jardin D'ete, located in the outdoor courtyard at the Brunswick, made for a refined summertime dining experience. This was one of several restaurants within the hotel.*

Park to Mount St. Vincent, down to Washington Square, and returned to the Brunswick.

Meant to be an elitist sport, it was Kane who made it possible for the general public to experience this affluent entertainment, if they could afford the three-dollar ticket. Kane's coach, called the *Tally-Ho,* departed from 26th Street and Fifth Avenue at 11 A.M. and arrived at the Arcularius Hotel in Pelham at noon. Passengers would disembark and enjoy a leisurely lunch and at 3 P.M. would start their return trip, arriving at the Brunswick

at 5 P.M. The coach could accommodate fifteen people, and trips were sold out six weeks in advance. An English guard looked after the passengers, collecting their fares and sounding the departure horn. Sixteen horses were used for the line, and they all sported bouquets of flowers at their left ears. On April 27, 1895, E. S. Martin said of coaching, "Nobody takes you yachting for hire, but the coaching-man does something that is pretty much analogous to it, and does it out of devotion to the sport."

The logistics of establishing the Coaching Club just one short block from Madison Square Garden cannot be overlooked. Madison Square Garden was built primarily to house the horse show. During the show the streets were resplendent in blue violets and yellow chrysanthemums, the official colors of this yearly event. Window displays on nearby streets handsomely displayed stirrups, crops, whips and other riding paraphernalia.

78 *Carriages of the Coaching Club depart from the Brunswick Hotel on Fifth Avenue. In the background, the park on the left and the Fifth Avenue Hotel on the right are clearly visible.*

79 *The* Tally-Ho *in the collection of the Museum of the City of New York.*

FROM RESIDENTIAL TO COMMERCIAL

It appears that the row of brownstones on Madison Square North was never altered for commercial use. Instead, by the turn of the century they were leveled three and four at a time and replaced by a series of commercial office buildings offering wonderful views of the park and the soon-to-be Flatiron Building. In 1896 the Brunswick Hotel closed its doors, and on its site in 1906, a twelve-story building by Francis H. Kimball and Harry R. Donnell was constructed of redbrick and limestone in the Renaissance Revival style, maintaining its predecessor's name. Brentano's bookstore and the fancy grocer, Park and Tilford were two of the early ground-floor tenants. Eventually the building filled with showrooms representing hundreds of manufacturers of porcelain, glass, ceramic, silver and the like from all over the world. Several times a year, thousands of buyers descend on this building to place their holiday orders. Today the building, whose main entrance is on Fifth Avenue, is simply referred to as 225 Fifth, or the Gift Building. On its park side it occupies numbers 1–9 East 26th Street. Adjacent to it is 11–13, a twenty-story office building built in 1912. Its ground floor is occupied by the International Silver Company, Towle Silversmiths, and Wallace Silversmiths.

80 *The Brunswick Building at the corner of 26th Street and Fifth Avenue. The traffic tower in the middle of Fifth Avenue afforded those in charge of traffic control a view up and down the avenue and a safe haven from which to alter the traffic lights on the busy, then two-way, thoroughfare.*

The office building at number 15 East 26th Street, also twenty stories and built in 1910 by Maynicke and Franke, was to become a most popular address for both the young and the old. It was here that Lionel Trains decided to establish its corporate headquarters, and it was said that in December this was as close as one could get to being at the North Pole. The first layout was built in 1926 and changed in detail from year to year and in basic design five times in the thirty-six years that Lionel was located at this address. One of the most popular model-train layouts opened in 1949 and was created with O gauge; it could be seen there until 1957, when it was replaced by the even more impressive Super O layout. In time Lionel was to acquire its rival, Gilbert's American Flyer Trains, featured for many years at the nearby Gilbert Hall of Science diagonally across the park (fig. 63). The Lionel showroom eventually moved to the Toy Center at 200 Fifth Avenue. In 1993 renamed the Madison Square Building, number 15 underwent a major renovation. Among its business tenants is StructureTone

a company whose efforts played an enormous part in the 1999-2001 restoration program of the Metropolitan Life Insurance complex of buildings.

A small five-story brick structure at number 21, the Chapman Building, is today home to a home furnishings showroom. An art gallery and other small businesses occupy the upper floors. Its small scale is exaggerated even more, as it appears sandwiched between its two towering neighbors. A rather interesting L-shaped multistoried office building at number 23 extends to 27th Street, wrapping around its corner neighbor at 26th and Madison Avenue. This

81 *Number 11-13 East 26th Street, under construction, is flanked by the Brunswick Building to its left and number 15 to its right. Carriages, now horse and horseless, await fares on Fifth Avenue.*

82 *The surviving brownstone home of Benjamin Field as it stood between its two towering neighbors.*

OPPOSITE
83 *Lionel's Super O layout.*

84 *The original home of the ASPCA at the corner of 26th and Madison Avenue. Two doors west, the diminutive Chapman Building has replaced the brownstone holdout.*

building today maintains its original classical entrance on the park, with a more modern interpretation of an entrance at 60 Madison Avenue. The architectural offices of Maynicke and Franke maintained their design offices here. The firm was responsible for several buildings on the square, including the Toy Center Building at 200 Fifth Avenue.

At the northwest corner of 26th Street, at number 50 Madison Avenue, an elegant four-story building by Renwick, Aspinwall & Owens, was erected for the ASPCA in 1896. An elaborate one-story entablature of the ASPCA symbol, which was part of the building's third-floor facade, has now been removed, along with a covered-portico entrance upon which were engraved the words "The American Society for the Prevention of Cruelty to Animals." At the time it was built, it faced Madison Square Garden, home at certain times of the year to the horse and dog shows and the circus. These animals, no doubt, were well looked after. Currently occupied by a real estate firm, the building will soon be rezoned for residential living and converted into several luxury apartments, some with perfect park views.

LIONEL

Referred to as "the biggest little railroad in the world," this Super O layout installed in the Lionel showroom at 15 West 26th Street was a must-see for every child. Completed in 1957 for the annual Toy Fair, the layout was designed by Jack Kindler, who created the track plan and supervised its construction. Here, he looks over his masterpiece from the control tower. It was the attention to detail created in this miniature world that was so appealing—like the drive-in movie theater and the tug boat in real water seen in the foreground of this installation to the far right and left respectively.

4

MADISON SQUARE EAST

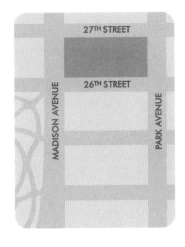

THE DEPOT

In 1832 the New York and Harlem Railroad moved its terminal, located at Prince and Center Streets, uptown to take over the entire block northeast of Madison Square Park between Madison and Park Avenues and 26th and 27th Streets. A low building with a single gothic tower housed a combination passenger depot, car barn, and freight and horse shed. Passengers boarded the horse-drawn cars and were transported from the depot up Park Avenue, via the underground tunnel between 33rd and 40th Streets that had been built in 1837. At 40th Street the cars were attached to locomotives for their trip out of town. They were returned to the Madison Square depot location in the same manner. (One made his or her way in and out of the city from this location in this fashion until the opening of Grand Central Station in 1871, with the combining of the Harlem, New York Central and Hudson River Railroads by Cornelius Vanderbilt.)

The old depot remained vacant until 1873, when its lease was taken over by P. T. Barnum for his "Monster Classical and Geological Hippodrome." Under a tent in the depot's open area, Barnum charged one dollar admission, and 15,000 people at a time were presented with outdoor shows that included chariot races, waltzing elephants, Arabian horses, Japanese tumblers, tattooed men, cowboys and Indians. To protect his tents, brick walls were erected and covered by a makeshift roof. Because of its central location at the time, the converted depot grew into a flourishing entertainment center, attracting patrons of the nearby grand hotels and restaurants.

OPPOSITE

85 The second Madison Square Garden designed by Stanford White opened in June 1890 and graced the east side of the Park. To the right of the Garden, at the southeast corner of 26th Street, is the Jerome Mansion.

86 The New York and Harlem Railroad depot as seen from the northeast corner of 27th Street and 4th Avenue (Park Avenue) looking west. The spire of the Madison Square Presbyterian Church is seen in the distance.

GILMORE'S GARDEN

Barnum soon realized that he could not maintain his spectacle in the cold arena through the long winter months, so in 1874 the lease was auctioned off to Patrick Gilmore, a noted military bandleader who, being quite a showman himself, put together a varied series of entertainments that included the revival meetings of Dwight L. Moody and Ira D. Sankey, temperance meetings, flower shows, and beauty contests and hosted Barnum's traveling circus when it came to town. He renamed his place of entertainment Gilmore's Garden and during the summer

months transformed the interior into spectacular gardens with fountains, statues, potted azaleas and various exotic plants set along graveled paths, filling the same environment where elephants and lions had made their way only a few weeks before. Tables were set and refreshments served while patrons were entertained by the likes of Theodore Thomas and his orchestra and Gilmore's well-known band. In 1877 he introduced the first Westminster Kennel Club Show, and it was in fact one of the canine show's executives, W. M. Tileston, who in 1878 picked up Gilmore's expired lease and kept the arena functioning by booking a variety of sports such as tennis, archery and riding.

Cornelius Vanderbilt had died in 1877, leaving his son William K. Vanderbilt with, among other holdings, the properties of the old depot on Madison Square. The younger Vanderbilt decided he would continue to rent the premises to various specialty shows, such as the circus and dog shows, but the main use of the complex would be as an athletic center. He officially renamed the arena Madison Square Garden, combining the name of the park, "Madison Square," with the "Garden" of Gilmore's venture, and reopened it Memorial Day 1879.

THE FIRST MADISON SQUARE GARDEN

The opening event featured a band concert given by Mr. Harvey B. Dodworth, the Garden's musical director. The *Times* stated: "The Garden has been fitted up with all the appliances for the enjoyment of visitors, and presented a brilliant spectacle last night. An immense audience was present, the boxes and seats along the sides being fully occupied, while the seats in the body of the building and the promenade were crowded. . . ."

It appears that Vanderbilt, applying some cosmetics to the interior, did not pay much attention to the structure itself. In February 1880 he hastily added an additional story to the newly named Garden's west facade along Madison Avenue, just before one of its biggest events, the Arion Masquerade Ball. A few months later, on April 21, during a benefit for the Hahnemann Hospital, festivities came to an abrupt halt when tragedy struck. Two thousand people were in attendance when a portion of the western wall caved in. Three people were killed instantly and twenty-two people were injured.

87 *P. T. Barnum brings his "Monster Classical and Geological Hippodrome" to the converted depot.*

88 *Glimpses of the grand interior space of Gilmore's Garden with its lush plantings and fountains and details of some of its offerings.*

Later that year, seeing the eventual need to replace the structurally unsound arena, Barnum conceived yet another of his grand schemes for this site. He formed the Barnum Museum Company (to which Vanderbilt gave his financial support) and proposed a new hippodrome. He based this plan on his successful American Museum, which had been located at Broadway and Ann Street from 1841 to 1865. It had stood on two city lots. Barnum's new grander plan for this site at Madison Square was to cover an entire city block, or the equivalent of thirty-four city lots. Almost ten years prior to Stanford White's Garden, the proposal's physical description outlined in an 1880 *Harper's Weekly* (fig. 90) matched almost detail for detail the concept for the future Madison Square Garden. It would have housed an arena; a zoological institute; aquaria; museum; opera house; lecture, exhibition and concert halls; and a tropical roof garden. Deemed too ambitious at the time, his plan was never carried out.

Despite this, Barnum was responsible for keeping the converted depot, now called Madison Square Garden, alive with his circus, which he faithfully brought to town each year. In 1882 he purchased Jumbo, the twenty-two-year-old African elephant, from the London Zoo for $10,000. It took sixteen horses to pull him on a flatcar from the dock to Madison Square Garden, and it took Barnum just three days to recoup his newest investment. The annual march of the elephants through the streets of New York City to their performance destination on Madison Square was to become a yearly sign that spring had arrived.

While Vanderbilt deliberated future use of his Garden, he booked six-day marathon bicycle races and boxing exhibitions. Boxing had been outlawed in 1856 and was not made legal as a spectator sport until 1920. Promoters, however, were able to put on "illustrated lectures on pugilism" to circumvent the law, although the police were never far from ringside to make their own judgment calls. John L. Sullivan, a heavyweight champion of the day, appeared at the Garden fighting Tug Wilson in a four-rounder on July 17, 1882. Sullivan's opponent had accepted the challenge under the agreement that any fighter still on his feet after four rounds would collect $1,000 and half the gate receipts. Wilson managed to avoid the grueling punches and made out quite well, in that the event drew huge crowds and more than 10,000 fans were turned away at the door.

89 *The depot, officially named Madison Square Garden, as it appeared in the 1880s.*

Madison Square Garden became the official site of the annual Horse Show in 1883, but unfortunately, even this spectacular event — along with the circus, the fights, the flower shows, the cattle shows, and the masked balls — was not enough to keep the garden open during the dark cold winter months. The enterprising Vanderbilt tried to beat these harsh conditions by flooding the main floor and creating a huge ice-skating rink, but sudden thaws soon put an end to this idea, so plans turned to replacing the existing structure with a new building.

By 1885 Vanderbilt had decided it was time to raze his "patched-up, grimy, drafty, combustible old shell," as the arena was described in *Harper's Weekly*. With this intent in mind, the Garden continued to struggle for the next few years. Several alternate uses were considered for the site, including

a large department store and an apartment dwelling. The innovative architectural team of Philip G. Hubert and James L. Pirsson, designers of the Chelsea Hotel on West 23rd Street, proposed an unusual thirteen-story courtyard apartment, consisting of six tiers of small two-story houses that would create a vertical village around a central green. On alternate floors, airborne walkways encircling the building like public sidewalks were to give free and open access to the parlor floors of each of the 240 two-story houses. This futuristic plan never materialized because buildings of this size were outlawed in 1885.

At the thought of losing the home for their annual event, horse show enthusiasts rose to the occasion. In 1887 Vanderbilt sold out to a group led by James T. Woodward that included Frank Sturgis, William Wharton, Hiram Hitchcock, an original proprietor of the Fifth Avenue Hotel and J. P. Morgan, the largest stockholder of the venture. Others with interest in this syndicate included James Stillman, Herman Oelrichs, James T. Hyde, Adrian Iselin, W. W. Astor, Edward Stokes, P. T. Barnum and Stanford White. Together they formed the Madison Square Garden Corporation and bought the site for $400,000. Over the next year, the group contemplated the future design of the new garden, studying submissions from Francis H. Kimball and Thomas Wisedell, among others. The former was the architect of the Brunswick Building (225 Fifth Avenue), the latter the architect of the Madison Square Theater on East 24th Street. The job was to go to McKim, Mead and White.

A *Harper's Weekly* of the day commented:

Madison Square Garden owing to its happy location and what may be termed "goodwill" of the spot, arising from the habit of citizens to go there for amusements of various kinds, has been marked these many years as the place for some building of public entertainment much finer than the present structure. It was determined to erect a composite edifice embracing a hippodrome, theater, ballroom, restaurant, concert hall and summer garden, thus forming a sort of pleasure exchange or central palace of pleasure.

P. T. BARNUM

Phineus T. Barnum was one of New York's greatest showmen. He was able to put a spin on most any mundane idea or curiosity and turn it into commercial success. He showcased many of these oddities at his American Museum, first located at Ann Street and Broadway and then at Spring Street and Broadway. Both were destroyed by fire, the former in 1865, the latter in 1868, but not before he had made a name for himself as an innovative impresario. In 1871, Barnum and William Coup established what was to be the first three-ring circus. By 1873 Barnum was presenting his circus, among other things, at the then-abandoned depot on Madison Square.

Barnum's last circus show in the depot opened March 12, 1888, the day of the record-breaking blizzard. An event that usually drew thousands produced fewer then 200 persons. Barnum was advised by the newspaper reporters who managed to show up at the onset of the storm not to go on with the show. But being the showman he was, he persevered, sending champagne to the journalists' boxes.

THE MADISON SQUARE GARDEN OF McKim, Mead and White

The old depot building was demolished by July 1889. Stanford White took the project under his wing and created a Spanish Renaissance–style structure of yellow brick and brown and buff terra-cotta. He modeled the main part of the structure after the grand cortile of the Ospedale Maggiore in Milan and fashioned the tower after the Moorish Giralda in Seville, Spain. Some observers likened the structure to the Doge's Palace in Venice.

One of the most challenging aspects of its construction was its scheduled completion in less than a year. The Garden could only afford to miss one season of shows without getting into financial trouble. This resulted in a rigorous twenty-four-hour work schedule. Once construction started, at least one thousand men were at work at any given time. The deadline was met and the official opening took place June 6, 1890. Seventeen thousand people paid $50 to enter the Garden. They filled the arena and were entertained by a gala concert led by Edward Strauss and two grand ballets. Although there were six thousand permanent seats, thirteen thousand additional spectators could be accommodated on the arena floor, not to mention standing room. Everyone who was anyone attended the opening. Many of the invited guests were escorted to their seats by attendants dressed in uniforms of yellow adorned with white satin scarves and silver-buttoned red waistcoats designed by White himself. Even before the structure was completed, the building met with popular acclaim. *Harper's Weekly* described it as "unrivaled as a place for summer entertainments" Charles De Kay declared the building "a great gain to the city in every way."

Madison Square Garden was completed at a cost of three million dollars. It measured 465 by 200 feet and was 65 feet high, not including the tower. In addition to the arena, the main structure included a theater, concert hall, swimming pool, shopping arcade, meeting hall and roof garden. The ground-level arcade, running along 26th Street and Madison Avenue, was designed to cover the sidewalks for the comfort and convenience of gathering crowds. Because it was to cover a public walkway, special state legislation was required in order to execute the design.

The Garden Theater, which occupied the building's northwest corner at Madison Avenue and 27th Street, had two balconies and was to feature comic opera. It opened September 27, 1890, with a production of *Dr. Bill*. The roof garden opened May 30, 1892, to an audience of four thousand and became known for its vaudeville performances. The tower, which had originally been planned for Madison Avenue, was temporarily dropped from the plan for lack of funds and later relocated on the East 26th Street facade. It rose 249 feet, enclosing three sky-high promenades, one above the other, and was adorned by *Diana*, a figure created by Augustus Saint-Gaudens and said to have been the first nude sculpture to be displayed in the United States in a public place.

OPPOSITE

90 *P. T. Barnum with his proposal for a house of entertainment on the depot site on Madison Square, that was to rival his own early and successful American Museum.*

91 *White's Madison Square Garden, detailing the tower, the original partially clad 18-foot* Diana *and the roof garden with a few of its cupolas.*

Portions of the tower were open to the public. The lower part contained two staircases nine feet wide, one winding above the other, the westerly staircase rising to the concert rooms and ballrooms and the easterly one to the roof garden and cafe. The roof garden was screened by open colonnades and protected by a removable glass roof for summer weather. From here a stairway ran to the top of the tower. There were 602 steps from the sidewalk to the top. The tower, 200 feet from ground level, was divided into seven floors between the roof garden and the first loggia. The highest outlook was 300 feet above the sidewalk. An elevator that held twenty-three people went to the second loggia, and stairs led as far up as the observation platform, 289 feet above the street; another circular platform big enough for only two was directly below the feet of *Diana*. The final ascent was definitely worth the climb. To the south, one could see the Neversink lights below Sandy Hook; to the north, the view reached over Central Park and Harlem to the Palisades above Yonkers; to the west, the hills of Orange, New Jersey; to the east, Brooklyn and Long Island.

EVENTS AT THE SECOND MADISON SQUARE GARDEN

The following observations about Madison Square Garden by Rupert Hughes in his book *The Real New York* (1904) capture the variety, scope, and excitement of a bygone Madison Square Garden:

Madison Square Garden! How much that means to the New Yorker. It is the most New Yorkish thing in town. It is a compendium of the city life in one volume; and well it may be, for there is no other building in the world, to be sure, that houses one-half the gaiety and energy, or half the variety.

Madison Square Garden — Here he is brought as a child to see the Greatest Show on Earth on a greater scale than in any tent — though not so easy to crawl under. Playing so

important a part in the New York child's education, it is small wonder he loves it when he is grown. And it grows with him; for when the circus is over, he goes to the Dog Show . . . the Cat Show. Once a year the Garden calls in all the country cousins and farmers, real or amateur, to see the Poultry Show. When the New Yorker grows older he probably joins a regiment. The Military Tournament draws him to the Garden . . . each of the regiments is represented in the opening review. The Wild West Show . . . the famous six-day bicycle race takes place here annually, and all night long the benches are crowded with enthusiasts . . . they bear the grind with amazing indifference, except when a spectator offers a cash prize for a short race; then they brighten up and flash round like demons. There is the Sportsmen's Show, and the building becomes a great landscape, with all manner of wild places condensed into one medley. One year one end was a range of mountains, with real trees and real streams of water. The water turned two old-fashioned wheels and then cascaded into a big lake in the center

complete with waterfowl and fish hatchery. A one hundred fifty foot tank built over the arena boxes allowed for spectators to try their skill at fly-casting.

The Garden is versatile enough to include everything from a wrestling match to a religious revival and on to a Fashion Show, where styles are shown some months in advance . . . [and] the Horse Show, which fills the Garden for a golden, glorious week. It is a yearly parade of horse flesh and society flesh.

The humorists annually make game of the Horse Show because the people themselves are the show and the horses only an excuse. Boxes were outfitted with easy chairs and Persian rugs were auctioned each year for this event for as much as $3,000. It was also estimated that the typical grandame in attendance might wear a gown, jewels and a wrap totaling $13,000.

Then there is the new rival of the horse, the automobile; he too must have his show. He is noisier, smellier and more unruly, but a great toy for grown-ups that can afford to "see the wheels go round," can pay for breakages and don't mind dust, grease and outré perfumes.

In the Garden in the summer there is Venice. The center of the arena is the Adriatic Sea or a circular Grand Canal. You can cross on a bridge or you can make the grand tour in a gondola with a human gondolier and some Italians who do a barber's work by day and sing barber chords by night with much twittering of mandolins and a loud chanting of "Finiculi, Finicula." At the end of the Garden is a large orchestra by Mr. Duss, formerly from Economy, Pa. Besides plenteous music there are drinks.

Although prizefighting was still illegal, it continued to draw large crowds. On February 16, 1892, Gentleman Jim Corbett put on a three-round exhibition fight. He took on three opponents and beat them all. Later that year he won the heavyweight title from the aging John L. Sullivan.

THREE GRAND
PATTI
CONCERTS.

92 *Opposite: Fashionable spectators at the Horse Show in November 1896, congratulating a winner.*

93 *Opposite, below: Several fund-raising events were held at the garden for a monument to Ulysses Grant. On October 2 and 3, 1891, a colossal production of S. G. Pratt's* Allegory of the War in Song *was presented and is depicted here in* Frank Leslie's Illustrated Newspaper.

94 *Gondolas float in the re-created waterways of Venice.*

95 *A portrait of Adelina Patti as she appeared at the Garden on May 10, 12, and 14, 1892 in a musical and operatic festival, where she was joined by a chorus of 1,000 and an orchestra of 100.*

96 *Edison shows his latest inventions at one of the Garden's many themed shows.*

97 *An early automobile exhibits its extraordinary power on a specially devised ramp angled at a daring incline on the Garden's roof garden.*

DIANA

Stanford White commissioned Augustus Saint-Gaudens to create a work to top his impressive Madison Square Garden Tower. Saint-Gaudens fashioned a figure of Diana, the huntress, in copper, to serve as a rather provocative weathervane. Her nude figure, partially clad by a scant piece of drapery, rested on forty polished ball bearings about the size of billiard balls, which enabled her to turn freely. *Diana* was unveiled atop the Garden's Tower in November of 1891. A crowd gathered in the square to watch as a workman climbed to the top of *Diana*'s head and slowly worked his way down her shoulders, loosening the robes that covered her. When he reached the crescent at Diana's foot, she was totally exposed, and at 5:15 P.M. she was illuminated by more than 1,000 incandescent bulbs that surrounded her head and outlined her bow and arrow. With *Diana*'s exposure came a flurry of widespread controversy. Ironically, the city of Philadelphia, where she was eventually to make her permanent home, took the greatest offense of all.

Diana had originally been created at a height of 18½ feet. When she was set into place, both White and Saint-Gaudens found her to be much too large, and at their own personal expense replaced her with a more-refined thirteen-foot figure in 1893. The model for both versions, Julia Baird declared herself "Diana of the Garden." For the eighteen-foot sculpture, Saint-Gaudens made a model of her figure, for which she simply posed. For the thirteen-foot *Diana*, a plaster cast was taken directly from her figure. This was done in sections that were then sent to the foundry of W. H. Mullins of Salem, Ohio, to be enlarged and executed in gilded copper. Made in two molds, the pieces were placed together and hammered and welded.

With the new *Diana* in place, the original *Diana* traveled to Chicago in 1893 to be displayed at the World's Columbian Exposition. She was installed atop the Agriculture Building designed by Charles McKim. The design of the fair was a close collaboration between Daniel Burnham and Frederick Law Olmsted. After her appearance there, she remained in Chicago, this time upon the Montgomery Ward and Company Building. Later her head was exhibited at the Chicago Museum of Fine Arts.

Diana's perch high above the park gave her spectacular views of the island and beyond, including a very clear sighting of the other lady of the time, the Statue of Liberty, which had preceded *Diana*'s creation by only four years. O. Henry wrote about them both in one of his short stories, "The Lady Higher Up," in which the two women have a delightful conversation. In one exchange Diana remarked to Lady Liberty, "It must be awfully lonesome down there with so much water around you. I don't see how you keep your hair in curl . . . I think those sculptor guys ought to be held for damages for putting iron or marble clothes on a lady. That's where Mr. Saint-Gaudens was wise. I'm always a little ahead of the styles; but they're coming my way pretty fast. Excuse my back a moment— I caught a puff of wind from the north."

98 *The better-proportioned second* Diana *as she appeared close to the end of her reign high atop the Madison Square Garden Tower. By this time the winds had disrobed her completely stripping away the drapery that once billowed from her shoulder (fig. 91).*

99 *When the second* Diana *finally came down in 1926, she found a new home at the Philadelphia Museum of Art, where she has been prominently displayed ever since. At the removal of the statue in 1925, to the left of Diana is the Garden's Tex Rickard and Stanford White's son, Lawrence, who, like his father, studied architecture and went on to head the firm of McKim, Mead and White.*

100 *A cartoon published years before the tragic death of Stanford White on the roof garden of his beloved Madison Square Garden has Lady Liberty crying "Murder" as Diana points her bow towards the statue in the harbor.*

MISS LIBERTY CATCHING FIRST GLIMPSE OF DIANA ON THE NEW MADISON SQUARE GARDEN TOWER—"MURDER"

STANFORD WHITE'S GARDEN

Stanford White occupied seven floors in the middle of the tower and often attended the roof garden restaurant. Here he entertained many lovely young ladies, among them Evelyn Nesbit. At age fifteen, she had caught White's atten-

tion as one of the Floradora Girls, a group that performed quite regularly at Madison Square Garden. She became his companion and described his private studio in the tower as straight out of a scene from the Arabian Nights. One of his more eccentric acts, related some years later by Nesbit, was to drug and seduce her and place her on exhibit on a red velvet swing in a small apartment he kept over the rear of the F.A.O. Schwarz toy store on West 24th Street just off Broadway. (The toy store itself was located at 39–41 West 23rd Street from 1900–10.) She soon decided on a quieter way of life and sometime later met and married Harry K. Thaw, who wanted to know every detail of her relationship with White. With this acquired knowledge he became enraged and insanely jealous. His dislike for White had apparently also been spurred on by another event involving a party that Thaw was to have given at Sherry's in honor of Frances Belmont. The night before the party, while walking through Sherry's with a friend, Frances Belmont passed the table where Thaw and some of his men friends were socializing. Thaw ignored her. She was so incensed that she imposed upon her good friend Stanford White to throw a party for all the women who had been invited to Thaw's event. He responded to her request, and Thaw's party turned into a stag affair while the girls enjoyed themselves in White's room in the tower. Thaw thought that White was the instigator and set out to seek revenge.

102 *Evelyn Nesbitt, seen here in a provocative pose photographed by Gertrude Käsabier, was a frequent entertainer in the roof garden theater and caught the eye of Stanford White when she was only fifteen.*

Towards the end of June 1906, Mrs. White had gone to St. James to open the couple's summer home. White remained in the city to review details for the new Parkhurst Church, just two blocks south of Madison Square Garden at 24th Street and Madison Avenue. On June 25th, he debated whether to go to Philadelphia for a business meeting the following day but decided against it. That evening White took his twenty-year-old son, Lawrence, and his son's friend LeRoy King, both on vacation from Harvard, to dinner at Café Martin, the old Delmonico's at 26th Street and Fifth Avenue. They dined on the Broadway side, which had been converted into a Parisian cafe. Harry Thaw and Evelyn Nesbit were dining in Café Martin's main dining room with some friends at the same time. Thaw's back was to White, but Nesbit could not let this sighting go unnoticed and slipped a note to Thaw in a further effort to evoke his jealousy. After dinner White drove his son and friend to the Aerial Garden, a theater located on the roof of the Amsterdam Theater on West 42nd Street, to see *The Governor's Son,* written by and starring George M. Cohan. After dropping the boys off, White made his way to his beloved tower to catch a late roof-garden show, *Mamzelle Champagne,* a musical by

Edgar Allan Woolf and Cassius Freeborn. Since White was one of the show's investors, it was billed as one of the "best, brightest, and breeziest shows in town." Whether by chance or by Thaw's compulsive need to stalk White, Thaw and Nesbit were in attendance that evening when White arrived. They were seated at the rear of the theater and White was seated by the stage for a while in the company of the Garden's caterer, Harry Stevens. Towards the end of the second act, the chorus girls, in pink tights, danced around a mammoth bottle of champagne as Harry Short sang, "I could love a thousand girls." At about 11 P.M., Thaw and his party got up to leave. They were almost out of sight when Thaw reappeared, walked up to White and shot him three times in the head at close range. At this moment the chorus girls were singing, "I challenge you to a duel," and for a fleeting moment the audience thought the activity surrounding the disruption might be part of the act. It quickly became apparent that, instead, they had just witnessed a horrible crime.

103 *Sketch of the shooting of Stanford White by Harry Thaw that appeared in the* New York Herald, *June 26, 1906. Details of the incident filled the front page of most newspapers for days.*

Thaw's trial drew almost more attention than White's death. It seemed that it was more important for the *Herald* and the *World* to print as scandalous a story as they could about White's womanizing so they could sell the highest number of papers. This unfair publicity led to a deadlocked jury. A second trial was held in 1908, and this time Thaw was found guilty by reason of insanity and was sent to the Matteawan Hospital for the Criminally Insane in New York. According to the book *Prodigal Days*, which was written twenty-eight years after the shooting, Nesbit related that Harry Thaw had planned this murder very carefully in order to ruin White's reputation. Nesbit's marriage to Thaw had always been quite rocky and ended in divorce soon after Thaw's release from the hospital. Surprisingly, very few of White's supporters spoke out on his behalf. Correspondent Richard Harding Davis came to his defense in an eloquent and supportive piece written on August 8, 1906, for *Colliers.* As a result, some of Davis's books were banned.

The Garden after White

White's aesthetic presence in the garden was sorely missed. The lack of maintenance was evident and the shine soon wore off. Despite its accolades, White's Madison Square Garden was never a tremendous commercial success from the time of its opening. It lost $18,000 the first year, $16,000 the second. Part of its problem was attributed to the death of P. T. Barnum in 1891, shortly after the new Garden opened. With the exception of four or five good years, the Garden showed a deficit every season until it was sold in 1908. Operating expenses were about $20,000 a month, which few shows brought in. Another unfortunate venture within the Garden was the beautifully designed restaurant located on the building's southwest corner. It seemed as if no reputable caterer wanted to take on this business because of its demanding and varying menus influenced by the events. For instance, during the Horse Show there might be a request for lobster a la Newburg and champagne, and the next day, with the circus or prizefights billed, a call for frankfurters and beer. Both Sherry's and Delmonico's were offered the site rent-free, and both declined. In 1908 the Garden was put up for sale and bought by the F and D Real Estate Company, with a mortgage secured by the New York Life Insurance Company. In 1913 ownership went to the insurance company.

Shortly before this, in 1911, George Lewis (Tex) Rickard, master showman, fundraiser and boxing promoter, came to the Garden. His forte was promoting boxing. By 1920, with the legalization of boxing, Rickard staged a successful event in which Jack Dempsey won one of the first legal fifteen-round bouts. Rickard's flair for promotion momentarily reversed the Garden's downward financial state. Using his showman skills and emulating the early attempts of Vanderbilt to attract a crowd, he flooded the arena and turned it into a swimming pool one summer. He offered evenings of music and dance after some of the sporting events as a ploy to help fill the house. Even though these PR attempts were somewhat fruitful, his presence came a bit too late to save the Garden. The impending plan to make this site the future home of the New York Life Insurance Building was about to become a reality.

Madison Square Garden had stood on this site for thirty-five years. The *New York Times* said, "It was the place where sports, society and politics met on common ground." A sportswriter wrote of Madison Square that it was "not a building but a state of mind." In 1894 Marianne Griswold Van Rensselaer commented in *Century* magazine that Madison Square Garden "asserts itself without rival. Nothing else in all New York has done so much to dignify, adorn, and enliven its neighborhood; nothing else would be so severely missed by all New Yorkers were ruin to overtake their dearest architectural possession." Rupert Hughes, commenting on the Garden and its tower in *The Real New York,* said:

> . . . whenever a hint of tearing it down has been whispered, a million voices have gone up against the sacrilege. Turn it into a temple, a post-office, anything; but keep it erect so long as the town holds beauty in esteem.

"What London would be without St. Paul's, or Paris without the Arc de Triomphe," said Blake, "that is what New York would be without Madison Square Garden."

The garden closed its doors on May 5, 1925. A crowd of 10,000 attended a heavyweight bout between Sid Terris and Johnny Dundee. Ring announcer Joe Humphreys emotionally bid a sad farewell with the playing of taps and the words "Farewell to thee, O Temple of Fistiana. Farewell to thee, O sweet Miss Diana."

The third Madison Square Garden opened on November 28, 1925, at its new location on the site of an old trolley barn between 49th and 50th Streets and Eighth Avenue. It remained there for about forty-three years, when it moved several blocks south to Eighth Avenue and 33rd Street, where the fourth and present Garden opened on February 11, 1968. The newly constructed building for the fourth Madison Square Garden was, ironically, built on the site of the much-acclaimed Pennsylvania Station, another McKim, Mead and White project. With each of its moves, it took with it the Madison Square name but none of the Garden's original aura that White had worked so hard to create.

Some years later, in the December 1928 issue of *Arts Magazine,* Harold Steinen mourned the loss of Madison Square Garden when he wrote, "It was a gracious building, with a lovely tower and on top a most alluring huntress. It was skillfully wrought and assembled by Stanford White and his group

104 *The Garden had become a popular spot for political rallies and was utilized by both the Democrats and Republicans who maintained their headquarters in hotels across the park. In 1892 Grover Cleveland made the most important speech of his political career at the Garden, after which every major party nominee appeared there well into the 1920s. Although it played host to all these candidates, it had never housed a national convention until 1924, when Rickard offered the Garden rent-free to the Democrats for the Democratic National Convention.*

105 *A souvenir from a political gathering in support of Al Smith in 1924.*

of artists to prove to New Yorkers how desirable it was to put beautiful buildings in their parks because that was the proper and educated way to behave. The need for some sort of culture, however brief, was real, and the fertile spirit of Stanford White was ideally suited to the task of importing culture wholesale."

THE NEW YORK LIFE INSURANCE BUILDING

Cass Gilbert was awarded the commission to design the new home for the New York Life Insurance Company. The imposing building was erected by the real estate company of Starrett Brothers over a two-year period from 1926 to 1928 at a cost of $21 million. Gilbert, who had worked in the offices of McKim, Mead and White, had made a concerted effort to salvage parts of White's Garden and tried to save part of the tower to utilize on another one of his commissions. His attempts failed and the building was demolished.

Gilbert's final design for the structure was considered to be an imposing and satisfactory solution to the problems that were presented to him, these being a modern office building, designed under the city's setback law, with the opportunity to build upon an entire city block. Following a trend toward simplification in architecture, Gilbert's detailing on New York Life was much freer than on his Woolworth's Building.

The new thirty-four-story building rose 617 feet and was designed with three setbacks, the first occurring at the fifth floor and the second at the fourteenth floor. The third setback on the twenty-sixth floor occurred on the east and west wings only. The central portion was a sheer rise from the thirteenth floor up to and including the thirty-fourth story. The largest order of Indiana limestone ever utilized in a single building was used throughout the facade, with solid-bronze frame and sash in its 2,180 windows. The interior arcade at street level is reminiscent of White's covered sidewalk arcade. The lobby ceiling is coffered with very large hanging lamps and doors of ornate bronze. Cass Gilbert referred to this architectural design as "American perpendicular," affording outside exposure to all offices in the upper portion of the building.

With the completion of the building came an opportunity to contrast this new structure with the old Madison Square Garden. This subject was covered in the December 1928 issue of *Arts Magazine*. The New York Life Building was referred to as "a handsome gift done up in a gothic wrapper." The building was referred to in the 2000 *AIA Guide to New York* as "limestone renaissance at the bottom, birthday cake at the top."

106 *The demolition of Madison Square Garden in 1926.*

107 *Prior to the appearance of the New York Life Insurance Building on Madison Square, a rather spectacular proposal for a skyscraper church, the Convocation Tower, was made in 1921 by Bertram Grosvenor Goodhue. The plan, considered one of Goodhue's highest achievements for the short-lived Inter-Church World movement, was to be a structure that was to rise eighty stories above the park. Church steeples, once so prominent in the early skyline, were now hidden by the emerging skyscraper buildings. The idea of incorporating the church into these tall structures became a way for commercial tenants, intended to occupy the upper floors, to support the increasing expenses of the growing church while providing them with high visibility.*

Cass Gilbert's final design for the New York Life Insurance building was nicknamed 'The Cathedral of Insurance.'

108 *Gilbert produced three separate design solutions for the New York Life Insurance Company. One of the proposals was a tower structure that protruded from a sphinx-like base. Although the tower was of different proportions from the Metropolitan Life Insurance Tower, its proximity would have been disturbing.*

80

REMEMBERING THE OLD MADISON SQUARE GARDEN

In a 1927 Valentine manual, *New York in the Elegant Eighties*, H. I. Phillips laments the loss of Madison Square Garden. Although sorely missed, Cass Gilbert's newly erected New York Life Insurance Building was to gain landmark status by the 21st century.

Madison Square Garden
Used to stand there
On the site of that
Skyscraper!

There's no band playing now,
No roaring of "wild and fee-ro-cious
Beasts of the jungle,"
No barking of dogs,
No chatter of monkeys or
Delegates to a
National convention.

In Office 157, first floor,
Where a bald little man
Sits dozing over "Flitcraft's Manual
Of Insurance Rates," scribbling
Figures and yawning
And taking pills out of a

Round box for his dyspepsia,
Stood the very ring where
John L. Sullivan battered
Down Slade, "The Maori,"
Dominick McCaffery and
Charlie Mitchell.
There Fitzsimmons
K.O.'d Gus Ruhlin. There
Corbett met McCoy,
Walcott met West,
Langford fought Jeannette,
Dixon fought Plimmer,
McCarthy fought Willard.
There, where that filing
Cabinet stands, Big Bill
Brennan fell when Dempsey
Hit him a blow so hard it
Sent an Irishman to a
Jewish Hospital!
There by the elevator shafts
Cheyenne Jake used to rope
Twelve racing cowboys abreast!

Up on the third floor in
Room 3267, the Board of
Directors of the International
Apricot Packing Corporation
Are in conference
In precisely the space and
Altitude in which
"The Girl of a Thousand
Whirls . . . Mlle. Dolores Lamaraletta"
And "The Peerless Queen of

Aerial Gymnasts, Miss Lilian
Leitzel," defied the
Laws of gravity
In pink tights!

There where Abner S. Wogg
Chairman of the Board, sits
Thumbing an annual report,
Ernie Clark of the
Clarkonian-Nelson Troupe
Used to take off
From his trapeze in his
"Triple somersault and reverse
Flight through space
Risking life and limb!"

Far up on the eighth floor
Miss Arabella Snodgrass
Public typist, is humming
"All Alone," at her desk,
Little dreaming that there
At her feet Stanford White was
Killed!

A skyscraper, eh?
No clowns, no fight champs,
No cowboys, Cossacks,
Midgets, sword swallowers,
Bearded ladies, gunmen,
Pickpockets, bootleggers,
Grand dames, actors,
Actresses, chorus girls,
Bike riders, gentlemen,
Dog fanciers.

No laughter of children,
No rumble of chariots,
No booming cries of
"Uppercut 'im Packy!"
No excitement, no thrills.

A skyscraper twenty-eight
Stories high and with 1,000 offices!

Well, what of it?
There isn't a kick in
A whole block of 'em.

Home Office Building of the New York Life Insurance Co.

By the 1950s, the building's distinctive pyramid shape gold leaf roof had been worn away and its copper base had disintegrated due to chemicals in the city's atmosphere. In 1956 the tower was sprayed with plastic roofing as a temporary measure to halt further deterioration. Carson, Lundin and Shaw were asked to come up with a permanent plan its restoration. The roof was refaced by the Turner Construction Corporation with gold-color ceramic tile and a new twenty-ounce lead-coated copper fleche. In 1966 Rambush, one of the few surviving handcraft studios in the country (founded in 1898 in New York City), was commissioned to gild the lacy finial and the four smaller turrets that surround the top of the golden pyramid. The results: a roof that catches and reflects the sunlight by day and by night is one of the more easily recognized shapes on the city's illuminated skyline. In 1987 Rambush also designed and fabricated the exterior sidewalk lanterns inspired by the massive lanterns in the entrance vestibules.

109 *Cass Gilbert's bold design for the New York Life Insurance Company.*

NYC
LANDMARK

NEW YORK LIFE
INSURANCE
COMPANY

51 MADISON AVENUE

OCTOBER 24
2000

MADISON SQUARE EAST—27TH TO 28TH STREETS

In 1963, in need of more office space, the New York Life Insurance Company expanded one block north, and filled approximately two-thirds of the block between 27th and 28th Streets between Madison and Park Avenues. The building that fronts Madison Avenue was designed by the architectural firm Carson, Lundin and Shaw. Within the last few years, New York Life has leased about half of this space to Ziff Davis Media Inc.

THE JEROME MANSION

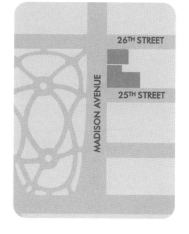

In 1865 Leonard Jerome built for himself a most imposing mansion at the southeast corner of 26th Street. Described as extravagant, careless and good-looking, he was a showy dresser and was famous for his fleet of racehorses. Originally a newspaper publisher in Rochester, he eventually associated himself with his older brother, Addison G. Jerome, and William R. Travis in a brokerage firm. The foundation for the Jerome fortune was made in the panic of 1857. Known for making and losing fortunes with great regularity, in a single drop of the exchange he was to lose $800,000 and eventually his great fortune of $6 million.

The new structure rose on an empty lot directly opposite Madison Square Garden when it was still a converted railroad depot. Jerome's complex consisted of three buildings running along 26th Street; the corner lot contained the house proper with a facade of continuous balconies on Madison Avenue facing the park. The six-story home of redbrick faced with marble was designed by Thomas R. Jackson (1826–1901), a London-born architect who came to New York in 1831 and worked in the office of Richard Upjohn. Jackson designed the Academy of Music on 14th Street and Tammany Hall. An early account from the *New York Times* in 1868 relates that the Jerome Mansion was originally built for the American Jockey Club, of which Jerome was a vice president. Jackson's design for the mansion, which was erected at a cost of $200,000, featured a mansard roof, extremely tall windows and double porches of delicate ironwork, making it an elegant addition to the park. A breakfast room for seventy, stables covered with walnut paneling, and rich carpets

110 *Looking south on Madison Avenue from the southeast corner of 26th Street. Dominating this corner is the Jerome Mansion, with its elaborate ironwork balconies facing the park and its main entrance on 26th Street. Its theater and stable are seen to the immediate left.*

costing $80,000 were only a few of its grand appointments. It was not unusual for Jerome to call upon Charles Ranhofer, head chef at Delmonico's across the park, to request on very short notice the catering of a dinner for a hundred or so guests. Ranhofer, who could handle several of these requests a day and still manage Delmonico's, would have the meal ready and served to perfection. A ballroom above the stables was where Jerome celebrated the completion of his new home. At this event, one fountain spouted champagne and another eau de cologne. On other occasions the ladies might have been apt to find jeweled bracelets in their napkins. The ballroom was later converted into a theater for six hundred guests, where the fashionable came to hear such entertainers of the day as Minnie Hawk, Adelina Patti, and Mrs. Purlie Lorrillard Ronalds. All had sought the attention of Jerome, but it was Mrs. Ronalds, admired by both August Belmont and Leonard Jerome, who was to be found more often in the latter's company and who remained his close companion throughout his life.

Jerome's wife, Clara Hall, came from a mixed background. Her father's family sported a coat of arms and her mother was one-quarter Iroquois Indian. Clara bore Jerome three daughters but soon left him and took the girls to live in Paris, amid the rumors of Jerome's many liaisons. One of their daughters, Jennie, grew up to marry the second son of the 7th Duke of Marlborough, Sir Randolph Churchill, in 1874 and soon thereafter became the mother of Winston Churchill.

Jerome spent only a few years in this magnificent residence. He spent much of his time thereafter traveling between New York and Europe, making the Brunswick Hotel his favorite haunt on his stays in the city.

The mansion was vacated by 1867, and one year later it was altered and rented to the Union League Club. This club was formed by New York Young Republicans to help the Union cause during the Civil War. One of the noteworthy events that took place here in 1869 was the convening of a group of prominent New Yorkers to form the Metropolitan Museum of Art. The art committee of the Union League Club held a public meeting at the club to discuss the establishment of a Municipal Museum of Art. As a result, the Metropolitan Museum of Art was organized in January 1870, with John Taylor Johnston as president and William Cullen Bryant and General John A. Dix as vice presidents. As early as 1856, John Taylor Johnston, living at number 8 Fifth Avenue, maintained an art gallery above the horse stables at the rear of his house. The gallery was opened to the public one day a week.

In 1881 the Union League moved to a new clubhouse built expressly for them at 39th Street and Fifth Avenue. The Jerome Mansion tenants that followed were the Turf Club in 1881, the Madison Club, which briefly occupied the mansion for part of 1883, in the same year the University Club, which stayed until 1899 when the Manhattan Club leased it. The Manhattan Club was the Democratic counterpart of the Union League Club. (It was at this location that the Manhattan cocktail was given its name.)

It was said that income from the rental of the Jerome Mansion, approximately $10,000 a year, provided part of Jennie Jerome's dowry. She (Lady Churchill) received income from the house until 1913, when it was sold to the Manhattan Club. In 1921, the year that Lady Churchill died, Winston Churchill received $150,000 when the club paid off a mortgage his mother held on the house.

THE UNION LEAGUE CLUB

An article in the *New York Times* from April 1, 1868, gives a descriptive account of the mansion's alterations to accommodate the needs of the Union League Club. It was related that

. . . the club monogram was placed on the large lamps at the main entrance on 26th Street. Within, no expense has been spared in furniture and appropriate ornamentation, and the various floors have been subdivided as follows: on the first floor are the visitors' reception-room, the reading room, the art gallery, the billiard room, the cloak and hat room, the bar and the ten-pin alleys. On the second floor is the theater, which it is proposed will be used for the more important meetings of the Club. . . . On this floor also have been constructed a number of private dining-rooms for Club members. On the third floor is the main parlor, looking on Madison Avenue, and from the windows of which the fine balcony running along that side of the building is reached. This parlor is fitted up in magnificent style, and hung around with portraits of patriots, dead and alive, and those of some friends of the Union abroad, and Cropsey's painting of "The Field of Gettysburg." Adjoining the parlor are the library, the trophy room and a fine, spacious saloon by which the theater is reached. On the three remaining floors are bedrooms, elegantly furnished, intended for the occasional accommodation of members. . . . In the basement are numerous offices, kitchen . . . and an engine to supply heat to the building and power when required. The remodeling and refitting of the interior cost $50,000.

THE STOKES FAMILY

Jerome's immediate neighbor to the south was James Stokes. He was a banker, real-estate owner, philanthropist and father of ten children. He moved his family to number 37 Madison Avenue in 1851 and built an adjoining brownstone for his mother at number 35. A hidden entrance connected the two brownstones on the parlor floor. Stokes, having preceded the Jeromes on the park by a few years, had kept his family cow in a stable just a few steps away on the then-empty corner lot at 26th Street.

Two of Stokes's daughters, Olivia, born in 1847 and her sister Caroline, born in 1854, grew up to continue the goodwill efforts established by the Stokes family. They traveled widely, wrote, and continued investing their time, energy and money in helping others. Some of their gifts to the city included St. Paul's Chapel at Columbia University and the open-air pulpit at the Cathedral of St. John the Divine. Caroline's love of horses was the inspiration for a unique fountain presented to the city and installed on Madison Square in August 1880 (fig. 23). It was a drinking fountain for both humans and horses and stood in front of Metropolitan Life's main building for more than seventy-five years. In 1911 the two sisters established the Phelps-Stokes Fund, endowed by Caroline with Olivia as its chief patron. It was a fund established for humanitarian and educational purposes. Among its primary objectives was the education of blacks in Africa and the United States. Olivia and Caroline were very close and continued to live at number 37 until 1902.

111 *The front parlor of number 37 Madison Avenue displayed some of the characteristic appointments of interiors during the 1850s and '60s. Among these were the marble mantel with its round-arched-opening, and the elaborate moldings where the walls and ceiling met. The refined furnishings include a recamier, carpets, decorative gaslight fixture and heavy drapes that frame the vertical panes of the front parlor windows, which overlooked the park. The many paintings, too many to hang, and the stacks of books on the table, express the family's interest in literature and the arts.*

112 *The two Stokes residences were classic examples of row houses surrounding the park. Number 37, on the left, was of Italianate style and number 35, to the right, was typical of the Anglo-Italianate style with its low 2-3 step stoop and a single round-headed window to the side. Its second-floor windows dropped to the floor, opening onto a cast-iron balcony.*

In 1910 James Stokes's son, Anson Phelps Stokes, a known chronicler of city events, compiled an extensive three-volume record of his family history. In one entry he reinforces his thoughts on the family's goodwill efforts by writing to them:

In times of prosperity, you may recall how many of your ancestors felt that the accumulation of money was not the highest of occupations, and devoted themselves to philanthropy, to disinterested public service in church and state, to the founding and care of schools and universities and charitable and religious institutions, to the amelioration of society, and to the dignity of life.

In 1881, the year his father died, Anson served on the committee for the Statue of Liberty's pedestal, and a few years later, in 1884, acted with his father-in-law as director of the Second National Bank while a replacement was found for its president, John C. Eno, accused of embezzlement.

The Stokes residences were replaced by the Madison Square Apartment House in 1902. The L-shaped structure, which was to become the Madison Square Hotel, wrapped around the old Jerome Mansion, occupying numbers 35 and 37 Madison Avenue and 38 and 40 East 26th Street. It was built for the Wyllys Company, a real-estate firm owned by Anson's sisters and his son I. N. Phelps Stokes, an architect and avid collector of prints and maps of New York. He produced the much-acclaimed *Iconography of Manhattan Island* (1915–28), considered to be one of the most comprehensive works on New York City. He and his wife, Edith Minturn Stokes, were the subjects of one of John Singer Sargent's notable portraits. I. N. Phelps Stokes was also a partner in the architectural firm of Howells and Stokes, which designed St. Paul's Chapel, one of his aunt's generous donations to the city.

THE MADISON SQUARE HOTEL, NEW YORK, N. Y.

THE MERCHANDISE MART

Although the Jerome Mansion had many tenants, it had only three owners: Jerome, the Manhattan Club, and Jackson A. Edwards, an electrical supply distributor who bought the house in the spring of 1965 for $600,000 with partner Herbert Fischbach, board chairman of Herbert Charles & Company, a real-estate concern. In September 1965 the house was designated a landmark by the New York City Landmarks Preservation Commission. It was considered a rare example of French Second Empire architecture. The new owners sued to have the landmark status removed so that their plans for a skyscraper could get underway. The Landmarks Commission searched for a suitable buyer for the house, an institution or professional group for which it could be an appropriate home. The commission had only a certain amount of time to find a buyer and failed to do so after many extensions.

The unspeakable took place on September 29, 1967. The new owners of the Jerome Mansion were given permission to proceed with demolition. They enlarged the building site by acquiring the adjoining Madison Square Hotel. There was an effort made by architect Roger Ferri to design a building that would in some way be sympathetic to its surroundings. What he conceived was almost a continuation of the park. He proposed a building that would maintain the street walls for the first four floors, then step back on the west side to allow for two-story-deep planting bins that would support a constantly changing landscape accessible from each office floor and be home to plants and animals native to the Hudson River Valley. His model even included grazing sheep! Unfortunately, the design chosen neglected any attempt to relate to the park and its surroundings. The new building had only one redeeming quality, which was purely unintentional: its dark-glass facade served as a stark background against which the impressive sculpture on the neighboring Appellate Courthouse could be clearly viewed.

113 The Madison Square Hotel accommodated the old Jerome Mansion by fronting Madison Avenue and 26th Street.

114 The forty-story New York Merchandise Mart at 41 Madison Avenue replaced the Jerome Mansion and Madison Square Hotel in 1965. Like 225 Fifth Avenue, showrooms fill this building, offering mostly tabletop items such as fine china, dinnerware and glass.

THE APPELLATE DIVISION OF THE NEW YORK SUPREME COURT

At the turn of the century a need for more courthouse space was growing. The appellate division was a fairly new addition to the state's court system and was in need of a building of its own. The new courthouse, along with several new courthouses built outside the civic center, would help meet the needs of the individual boroughs. Since the Appellate Court's work involved appeals from the Supreme Court, the Surrogate's Court and the Family Court in New York and Bronx

Counties, it also made sense for the Appellate Division to be located elsewhere. James Brown Lord was selected by the court to remodel a section in the old Arnold Constable Building at Fifth Avenue and 19th Street for the court's temporary use. They were so pleased with his solution that he was commissioned to design the Appellate Division's new home at the northeast corner of 25th Street and Madison Avenue.

Lord was a fitting choice for the design of the Appellate Courthouse in that both maternal and paternal grandparents of his were founders of law firms. After graduation with Princeton's class of 1879, he worked with the firm of William A. Potter, a leading church architect. In practice for himself, he designed several restaurants for the Delmonico family, the first at 44th Street and Fifth Avenue, followed by a restaurant for men only at the original Delmonico's site at William and Beaver Streets. Later in his career, Lord's design of the Yorkville Branch of the New York Public Library at 222 East 79th Street led to "establishing the character for Manhattan branch libraries: conceived as an elegant townhouse with light-filled rooms, it was the icon of humanistic reason and a refuge from the turmoil of the city" (New York 1900).

The design of the new courthouse on the park evoked the influence of Andrea Palladio, the noted architect of Vicenza, with its use of the columned porch and statuary. It was thought that the 25th Street facade, the main courthouse entrance, with its Corinthian order, might also have borne some resemblance to the residence of the Lord of Mayors in London by English architect George Dance, the elder. The interior walls in the main hall and courtroom are lined with Sienna marble and are detailed with fluted piers and Corinthian pilasters. The Empire City Marble Company supplied the exterior marble from North Adams, Massachusetts, and J. H. Shipway and Brothers finished the interior marble. Levinson and Just did the structural and decorative ironwork. The actual construction cost of the courthouse was $422,468, the statuary $157,000, and the mural painting $54,000, totaling well under the estimated $700,000 set aside. Charles T. Wills was the contractor.

It was Lord's plan for this building to incorporate great painting and sculpture as an integral part of the architecture. The theme would deal with the historical development of justice and law. The project was encouraged by the Municipal Arts Society, which had sponsored other similar endeavors, such as the decoration of rooms in the Criminal Courts Building on Centre Street. Edwin Howland Blashfield, who was to become one of the courthouse muralists, told the Society in 1893 that it was incidental which artists did the work of decorating a building. "The fact that the city would annually obtain a dignified and adequate work of art," he maintained, "is of weightier significance, but even this is unimportant by the side of the far greater fact that such a growth of art, art on a large scale, enhanced by architectural setting, will infallibly establish a standard and create a national faith in the national art." The National Society of Mural Painters prepared a program whereby artists chosen had to follow a general agreed-upon plan of decoration from first sketch to the finished mural in order to achieve a harmonious feeling. They had to adhere to a consistent figure scale and color scheme. John La Farge, dean of American mural painters and, ironically, a lawyer in his early years, was made arbiter to smooth out differences of opinion by the selected artists.

A number of talented sculptors were sponsored by the National Sculpture Society to execute the sculpture that was to grace the Appellate Courthouse's balustrade and exterior walls. An observer had said at the time that James Brown Lord was proposing a necessary marriage of the arts: "If built

JOHN LA FARGE

As a young man, La Farge's interests included law, history, religion, politics, music and art. In 1856, at the age of twenty-six and at his father's suggestion, he went to Paris to study painting. On the boat he met and apprenticed himself to a painter named Couture. After a three-week period he was released by his teacher, who immediately realized his student's talent. He took his instructor's advice and copied the masters. He spent a year in England and returned to New York to open a law office. A year later William Morris Hunt convinced La Farge to leave his law practice and move to Newport to pursue a career in painting. La Farge further experimented with stained glass and became a master of the art. In 1876 he worked with Henry Hobson Richardson on Trinity Church in Boston. In the '80s on a trip to Japan he developed an interest in Japanese art and the religion and philosophies of the East. In 1892 La Farge took up teaching and published some of his lectures, becoming a much-respected "great man" of the arts. La Farge helped Stanford White decide on a career in architecture as opposed to one in painting, and White later sought his expertise in choosing the final design for the Farragut Monument base in Madison Square Park.

APPELLATE COURTHOUSE SCULPTURE

MADISON SQUARE FACADE
(parapet, left to right)

1 **CHINESE LAW**– Confucius by Phillip Martiny

2 **PEACE** by Karl Bitter

3 **HEBRAIC LAW**– Moses by William Couper

(The four caryatids below the parapet.)

4 **WINTER, AUTUMN, SUMMER AND SPRING** by Thomas Shields Clarke

25TH STREET FACADE (parapet, left to right)

5 This figure of Mohammad by Charles Albert Lopez was removed in 1955, at which time all the figures were moved over one position to the west leaving the most easterly bay empty.

6 **PERSIAN LAW**– Zoroaster by Edward C. Potter

7 **ANGLO-SAXON LAW**– Alfred the Great by J. S. Hartley

8 **SPARTAN LAW**– Lycurgus by George E. Bisell

9 **JUSTICE** (above the Pediment)– Power & Study by Daniel Chester French

10 **ATHENIAN LAW**– Solon by Herbert Adams

11 **FRENCH LAW**– Saint Louis (Louis IX of France) by John Donaghue

12 **INDIAN LAW**– Manu, the mythical author of the Law of Manu by Augustus Lukeman

13 **ROMAN LAW**– Justinian by Henry K. Bush-Brown

MAIN ENTRANCE ON 25TH STREET FACADE (from left to right)

14 In the pediment: A group representing Triumph of Law by Charles Neuhaus. Depicted here are such symbols of law as the crescent moon, the ram, Father Time with his scythe, the owl, and tables of law.

15a, 15b Above windows within portico: Representations of Morning and Night, with a crescent moon and stars, and Noon and Evening, with bat with wings spread by Maximilian N. Schwartzott.

16a, 16b Seated statues flanking the main entrance: Force and Wisdom by Frederick Wellington Ruckstul. A quote for the former reads, "We must not use force till just laws are defied" and for the latter "Every law not based on wisdom is a menace to the state."

of marble, as you propose, with the sculpture all complete upon it, it will surely be one of the monuments of the city. I cannot impress upon you too strongly, to beg your committee that they allow you all the sculpture that you propose; it is its life and soul."

La Farge's job of keeping peace among the artists and their works of art for the courthouse interior was a bit more challenging than for the sculptures that adorned the exterior and stood prominently on their own or were enclosed within an architectural element. Many of the paintings — with their variety of compositions, styles and color — so closely juxtaposed to each other, could have created an impossible task to produce a unified effect. However, La Farge's success is evident as you walk through this uniquely harmonious space. Upon entering the main hall from 25th Street, one is encircled by a continuous frieze, the work of several artists. The frieze by H. Siddons Mowbray opposite the main entrance, entitled *Transmission of the Law*, shows the progress of law from Mosaic, Egyptian, Greek, Roman, Byzantine, Norman, and Common to Modern. On the left side is *Justice,* flanked by, among others, Willard Metcalf's *Mercy* on her left and *Law* on her right. On the right we see Robert Reid's *Justice* giving *Peace* and *Prosperity* to the *Arts* and *Sciences.* The south wall panels include, on the left, a seated figure of *Fame* surrounded by the *Arts,* also inspired by Robert Reid, and to the right, *The Banishment of Discord* by Metcalf. The spandrels of the main door contain the figures of *Equity* and *Law* by Charles Y. Turner.

The courtroom is partially lit by the impressive glow of the magnificent stained-glass dome of the Maitland Armstrong Company. The interior furnishings were created by the Herter Brothers. The

115 *The completed Appellate Courthouse as it appeared in the year 1900.*

three large panels on the east wall facing the dais are, from left to right, *The Justice of Law* by Edward E. Simmons, *Wisdom* by Henry O. Walker, and *The Power of the Law* by Edwin H. Blashfield. Behind the dais on the west wall is a frieze by Kenyon Cox entitled *The Reign of Law*. Flanking these on the north and south walls are sixteen panels by Joseph Lauber called *The Judicial and Other Virtues*. On the north wall, from left to right, are *Moderation, Veneration, Perspicuity, Eloquence, Reticence, Research, Unity,* and *Fortitude*. On the south wall, from left to right, are *Justice, Truth, Philosophy, Courage, Patriotism, Logic, Knowledge,* and *Prudence*.

It was Lord's job to orchestrate a total of twenty-four artisans, and this he did quite effectively with the help of La Farge's watchful eye. The courthouse was completed and occupied on January 2, 1900, and was Lord's last commission; he died in 1902. This structure today continues to maintain its distinguished presence on the park while also serving as a permanent collection of works by so many of the gifted artists and artisans of a bygone era. Their art adorned the ceilings and walls of some of the park's elegant hotels and restaurants, possibly graced several Madison Square mansions, were exhibited at nearby museums and galleries, and enriched the short-lived ceremonial arches that rose along Fifth Avenue near the Worth Monument.

There have been a series of restorations, the first occurring between 1954 and 1955, when the exterior was resurfaced, with Alabama Madre marble replacing the original Massachusetts marble, and the statue of Mohammed by

NYC
LANDMARK

APPELLATE COURTHOUSE
27 MADISON AVENUE

EXTERIOR
JUNE 7, 1966

INTERIOR
OCTOBER 27, 1981
MAIN HALL, COURTROOM,
AND LAWYERS' ANTEROOM

NEW YORK STATE AND
NATIONAL REGISTERS
OF
HISTORIC PLACES
1982

116 *Stained-glass dome in courtroom by Maitland Armstrong Company.*

117 *Murals on east wall of courtroom from left to right:* Justice of the Law *by Edward Simmons;* Wisdom *by Henry O. Walker;* Power of the Law *by Edwin H. Blashfield.*

OPPOSITE

118 *A proposal for the Supreme Court Building on Madison Square.*

119 *The Holocaust Memorial on the facade of the Appellate Courthouse annex.*

Charles A. Lopez being removed at the request of several Muslim nations that found it offensive to their religion, which forbids the representation of humans in sculpture and painting. When it was removed, all the other sculptures were moved over one space, leaving an empty bay on the eastern end. At that time a five-story addition was built on Madison Avenue. It carried no exterior decoration but was designed to harmonize with the existing courthouse.

In 1982 Rambusch was commissioned to restore the stained-glass dome that was broken, dirty and in danger of collapse due to structural faults in its initial 1900 installation. They removed, cleaned, repaired and reinstalled the twenty-six-foot-diameter dome. The structural fault was rectified by adding stronger rib supports. These were encased in molded-fiberglass strips of classical design. Once in place, the fiberglass was gilded, becoming an appropriate decorative accent while creating the correct support.

THE HOLOCAUST MEMORIAL

On May 22, 1990, a memorial to the *Victims of the Injustice of the Holocaust* was unveiled and became the first sculpture to be added to the courthouse since 1900. It was installed at street level against the northernmost part of the courthouse addition on the Madison Avenue facade. At the public ceremony held outside the courthouse, then-governor Mario Cuomo, then-mayor David N. Dinkins, former Mayor Edward I. Koch and presiding Justice Francis T. Murphy spoke. The ceremony opened with a fanfare for brass written by Ellen Levy and ended with a moment of silence. The monument, a six-sided half column that rises 27 feet from a

9½ inch concave base, was designed by Harriet Feigenbaum, whose design was selected from thirty-five submissions. The column is carved with images of flames, and a relief of an aerial view of the main camp in Auschwitz is worked into the base. The monument was made in Tuscany by the stone company of Walker and Zanger. Zanger's parents were refugees from Nazi Germany, and many of the workers at the fabrication shop of Menchini Guido and Fratello, where the sculpture was created, perished as punishment for their partisan activities. The installation and lighting were all donated. Justice Murphy said of the sculpture, "The Holocaust Memorial, now forever a part of this historic courthouse, shall stand as a reminder of past injustice impelling us to rededicate ourselves, daily, to the protection of individual freedom and dignity."

PROPOSAL

In 1909 plans were made to create a new home for the New York Supreme Court that would replace the New York County Courthouse (the old Tweed Courthouse) on Chambers Street. One of the sites would have covered the entire block between 24th and 25th Streets, directly opposite the Appellate Courthouse on Madison Square Park. The architectural firm of Howells and Stokes proposed a very grand and dramatic design scheme for a building, which at street level would have housed various offices and a library, while a nine-story tower set upon it would have contained the courtrooms. The site finally chosen was between Pearl and Worth Streets at 60 Centre Street at Foley Square, its present location.

A FEW PROMINENT FAMILIES

The two blocks between 23rd and 25th Streets on the east side of the park were also home to several distinguished New York families. The continuous line of brownstones was interrupted at the southeast corner of 24th Street by the Madison Square Presbyterian Church. On the southeast corner of 25th Street stood the residence of Peter Ronalds, who had been connected with the Lorillard family. On the same block but at the northeast corner of 24th Street was the house of John David Wolfe, a successful hardware merchant who was active in organizations having to do with improving conditions in the community. He married the daughter of Peter Lorillard. Their daughter, Catherine Lorillard Wolfe, won the title of "the great lady" by continuing her father's philanthropic activities and donating a great deal of money to Grace Church. Miss Wolfe also gave her magnificent art collection to the Metropolitan Museum of Art.

Adjoining the Parkhurst Church to its south at number 3 was the residence of William H. Appleton, who was prominently connected with the New York Life Insurance Company. On the corner of Madison and 23rd Street was the home of William Lane, a leading wholesale dry-goods dealer at the time. He sold his house to S. M. L. Barlow, a prominent lawyer who had one of the largest collections of Americana in the country. Mr. Barlow married the daughter of Peter Townsend, who lived on the south side of 23rd Street.

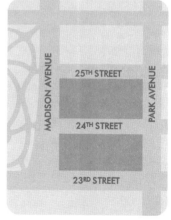

120 *The Madison Square Presbyterian Church with neighboring brownstone homes and the corner mansion of S. M. L. Barlow.*

MADISON SQUARE PRESBYTERIAN CHURCH

Directly across from the home of John Wolfe was the Madison Square Presbyterian Church. Founded in 1853 by William Adams, it was housed in a tall-spired brownstone Gothic structure. It was one of the wealthiest congregations in the country, made up of bankers, politicians, merchants and professional men. It was here that Theodore Roosevelt was baptized, on April 21, 1860, and later attended Sunday school. The Roosevelts, who lived nearby on East 21st Street, were members of the church, and Theodore Roosevelt Sr. served on the church's Mission Committee from 1859 to 1874. He was known to drop little Theodore off at the church on his way to teach a class at the Mission Sabbath School. Members of the Mission Committee, especially the chairman, were expected to attend Sabbath-evening services as well as weekly services at the mission.

Adams was succeeded by the colorful Dr. Charles H. Parkhurst, and the church soon bore the Parkhurst name. Between 1892 and 1894 Parkhurst led a campaign against citywide crime and police corruption. It was on Sunday morning, February 14, 1892, that he stepped up to the pulpit at his church on Madison Square and declared New York City thoroughly rotten. He pointed his finger at Mayor Hugh J. Grant, District Attorney DeLancy Nicoll, and four police commissioners. "Every step that we take looking to the moral betterment of this city," he charged, "has to be taken directly in the teeth of the damnable pack of administrative bloodhounds that are fattening themselves on the ethical flesh and blood of our citizenship." Grant challenged Parkhurst to prove his allegation. A week later the minister was unable to produce any evidence to back his accusations, although he had based his charges on undisputed newspaper articles.

Discouraged by not having his disclosures acknowledged, he sought the advice of commissioner merchant David J. Whitney, founder of the Society for the Prevention of Crime, a private organization of clergymen, merchants and lawyers. Whitney suggested that Parkhurst see firsthand the workings of the underworld and put him in touch with Charles W. Gardner, a private detective. Gardner would act as his guide, and John Langdon Erving, a young energetic member of the church, would accompany them. Gardner helped in their disguises, dressing Parkhurst in a dirty shirt, a baggy pair of black-and-white-checked trousers, a worn double-breasted jacket, and a tie made from the sleeve of an old flannel shirt. He then smeared the reverend's very distinguished whiskers with laundry soap, giving him a totally unkempt look. On March 5 they started their rounds of questionable locations in the city. At several brothels, the reverend was approached to pass some time with a number of prostitutes but managed to dodge their advances. On March 9 at the bar at the East River Hotel, they found two cops having drinks on the house. The detective got their badge numbers. On another sojourn they were taken to the Bowery and several concert gardens and brothels. On Elizabeth Street they were lured into a boarding house "for the most respectable policemen" in the city. In Greenwich Village entire blocks were filled with houses of prostitution. With the aid of four hired detectives, a total of 254 saloons were visited. Parkhurst spent about $500 on the investigation. Sunday March 13th found him at the pulpit once more, this time with tangible evidence to back up his allegations. He was unrelenting in his attacks on the alliance of Tammany Hall and the underworld. Tammany Hall was a political organization founded in 1788 that, over the years, grew corrupt and was known for freely accepting bribes for political and city appointments. Tammany had a regular scale of charges for police appointments.

121 *The outspoken Dr. Charles H. Parkhurst of the Madison Square Presbyterian Church. The building eventually bore his name.*

A patrolman would have to pay three hundred dollars for his job, a sergeant sixteen hundred dollars, and a captain of a profitable district perhaps fifteen thousand dollars. Police officials couldn't live decently on their official salaries, so to further their careers they freely accepted bribes from businesses in their assigned districts.

Finally the Chamber of Commerce asked the state legislature to investigate the city's police department. Clarence Lexow, a Republican senator, the chairman of the investigation of crime and corruption in New York City, was appointed to form a committee to continue Parkhurst's efforts. About seventy indictments were made against police officers — including two former commissioners, three inspectors, one former inspector, twenty captains and two former captains. For Parkhurst's efforts, many thought that an arch should be erected in Madison Square Park, that his birthday should be made a national holiday, and that New York should be renamed Parkhurst. These basically unrealistic proposals did evolve into a plan for yet another statue for Madison Square Park. In 1935 the *New York Herald Tribune* reported that a statue was being completed by Herman A. MacNeil and would be presented to the city and placed in Madison Square Park by the Society for the Prevention of Crime. The statue was part of a total plan to renovate the park that never occurred.

122 *The Metropolitan Life Insurance Company's first building on Madison Square at Madison Avenue and the corner of 23rd Street.*

123 *The main staircase within the Metropolitan Life Insurance Company's new building, modeled after the Paris Opera House.*

MET LIFE MOVES TO MADISON SQUARE

It was in the 1880s, with need for larger quarters, that Metropolitan Life Insurance Company decided to relocate its downtown offices to Madison Square. The decision by Met executives to move so far north was regarded as nothing short of adventurous. The entire two-block complex was built in fourteen separate stages and is best illustrated in the following breakdowns. The first — diagram A, (fig. 124) Met Life 1890–1918 — indicates the dates of the construction of buildings 1 through 9; and the second — diagram B, (fig. 131) Met Life 1919–2000 — indicates the last five phases of construction.

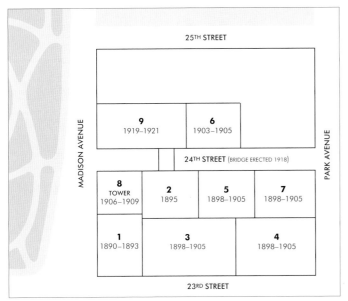

<table>
<tr><td colspan="3" align="center">25TH STREET</td></tr>
<tr><td>**9**
1919–1921</td><td>**6**
1903–1905</td><td></td></tr>
</table>

(Diagram A)

- 25TH STREET
- MADISON AVENUE
- PARK AVENUE
- **9** 1919–1921
- **6** 1903–1905
- 24TH STREET (BRIDGE ERECTED 1918)
- **8** TOWER 1906–1909
- **2** 1895
- **5** 1898–1905
- **7** 1898–1905
- **1** 1890–1893
- **3** 1898–1905
- **4** 1898–1905
- 23RD STREET

1– The first building of the complex was built at the corner of Madison Avenue and 23rd Street, adjoining the Parkhurst Church. It was designed by Napoleon Le Brun & Sons and built between 1890 and 1893. The early renaissance style of northern Italy was readily adaptable to the commercial requirements of the day and established the design motif for the many additions that were to follow. The high ceilings and large windows grouped in bays, characteristic of the Italian style, admitted an abundance of light to the massive masonry that encased the steel frame. Met Life continued to grow and, with some of its floors rented to other businesses, had to make a decision as to whether to take over the rental space or build an addition for its exclusive use. They decided on the latter.

124 *Diagram A — Showing the building program for the Metropolitan Life Insurance Company from 1890–1918.*

125 *The National Academy of Design at the northeast corner of 23rd Street and Fourth Avenue. Immediately adjacent to it on Fourth Avenue is the Lyceum Theater. The steeple of Madison Square Presbyterian Church is seen to the extreme left.*

2– In 1894 Met Life purchased the property located in the center of the south side of 24th Street extending 115 feet east of the first Madison Square Presbyterian Church. The entire home office was moved into this new twelve-story building.

3– Parcels of land adjoining the original building were acquired at this time, and a two-story addition was built in 1898, serving as a so-called "taxpayer."

4– With the next addition of the building complex at the corner of 23rd Street and Fourth Avenue in 1898 came the uprooting of the National Academy of Design, designed by Peter B. Wight (1863–65). Located at the northwest corner of 23rd Street, it was founded by Samuel Morse in 1826, and dedicated to

art education and the display of contemporary fine art. The adjacent Lyceum Theater and the cobbler shop of Augustus Saint-Gaudens's father, both located on Fourth Avenue between 23rd and 24th Streets, were likewise absorbed. The Lyceum was the very first theater to employ electricity for its auditorium and the stage. Thomas Edison invented new focusable lamps for the theater, and Louis C. Tiffany designed the special chandeliers for Edison's incandescent lamps. A young Saint-Gaudens took classes at the academy just a few short steps from his father's shop.

5– Construction on the fifth addition started in 1896 on the newly acquired land adjoining the 24th Street building.

6– Unable to wait for the acquisition of the remaining parcel of land at the corner of 24th Street and Fourth Avenue, the company purchased a site on the north side of 24th Street. On a plot 75 feet by 100 feet, a sixteen-story annex was erected between 1903 and 1905 to house the Printing Division, which occupied half the building upon completion. A two-story tunnel was built at this time to connect the annex with the main building at both the basement and sub-basement levels. The heavy ornamentation, so evident on the main building, was not used on the annex.

7– In 1905 the corner property of 24th Street and Fourth Avenue was acquired and developed, leaving the only remaining site on this entire block complex the Parkhurst Church. It had long been known that this corner would complete the original architectural scheme. Some kind of tower had been envisioned years before, in 1893, by then-president John R. Hegeman. In 1902 the first meeting between congregants and Met Life took place, where the church agreed to move directly across the street, from the southeast corner to the northeast corner of Madison Avenue and 24th Street. They were promised a grander structure with room for a much-larger congregation and a cash sum of $325,000. In 1903 McKim, Mead and White was selected as the architectural firm, and in 1904 a contract was signed with Charles T. Wills, who had been contractor several years earlier for the Appellate Courthouse.

A TOWER FOR MET LIFE AND A NEW CHURCH FOR DR. PARKHURST

Before Met Life was permitted to start work on the tower, the new church had to be built and ready for occupancy. It was only then that the old church could be demolished. Stanford White was put in charge of this project and it was to become one of his most favored projects and one of his last commissions. White used the church of Hagia Sophia (Istanbul) for inspiration. The dome of gold mosaic by Tiffany was illuminated by hidden lamps whose light bounced off the dome. The Tiffany studios also furnished the pews, altar furniture, organ case and stained-glass windows.

To make a bold statement on the park and in order for the church not to be totally overshadowed by its towering neighbors, White gave the church a slightly outscaled portico. Six imposing thirty-foot pale green granite Corinthian columns supported a pediment adorned with a cream and blue terra-cotta relief, designed by Adolph Weinman and painted by H. Siddons Mowbray, reminiscent of the work of Della Robbia. The structure was capped by a low green-tiled dome and topped with a golden lantern some 113 feet above the street.

The interior plan was based on a compact Greek cross, 74 feet by 84 feet. The sanctuary walls were simply treated with contrasting plain panels and areas of ornament. The facade of brick, and terra-cotta of light buff with the ornamental moldings of varying colors of yellow, moss green, light raw

126 *Stanford White's Madison Square Presbyterian Church, built directly opposite the original church at the northeast corner of 24th Street. Directly behind it stands the sixteen-story Metropolitan Life Annex Building, completed about the same time.*

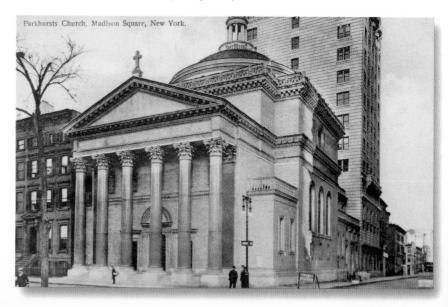

Parkhursts Church, Madison Square, New York.

umber, and blue-gray, formed delicate horizontal bands of color. This was apparently the first time that several colors had been used in architectural terra-cotta in the United States. White had worked long and hard with the Perth Amboy Brick Company to make both materials in differ-

ent hues. They perfected the method in 1903 and White used it liberally in this new project. The striking bold colors of the completed building earned it the affectionate nickname "The Church of the Holy Stein." This distinguished structure was given the Medal of Honor by the New York Chapter of the American Institute of Architects. For a very brief time, both churches stood side by side, the second church remaining on its new site for thirteen years until 1919, when Metropolitan Life bought the property for its North building.

THE MET LIFE TOWER

In 1909 Napoleon Le Brun designed the fifty-story Met Life Tower (phase 8) for the original site of the Parkhurst Church. The Met Tower was designed in the Italian Renaissance style and was based on the campanile of St. Marks Square in Venice. Having surpassed the Singer Tower in height, it held the record as the world's tallest building for four years and was once considered one of the Seven Wonders of the World. It lost its record in 1913, when it was exceeded in height by the sixty-story Woolworth Building. The tower, which runs 75 feet along Madison Avenue and 85 feet on 24th Street, rises 700 feet above the sidewalk and projects about 5 feet beyond the main building, helping to accentuate its height. The architectural detailing of the original adjacent Met Life Building was used throughout. A loggia of open arches, crowned by a strong entablature and balustrade, are located between the thirty-first and thirty-fifth floors. At the thirty-sixth floor the walls of the tower are set back, creating a massive base for the pyramidal spire that supports the octagonal turret and a golden dome. An observation deck was located on the forty-first floor. At the top an octagonal lantern, eight feet in diameter, sheds powerful electric flashes that mark the hours, working in tandem with one of the grandest features of the tower, its monumental clock.

127 *For a brief while, the old and new churches stood side by side while plans were drawn up for the Metropolitan Tower.*

128 *Between 1906 and 1909, the Metropolitan Tower slowly took shape, rising 700 feet above Madison Square Park.*

129 *The completed bell tower added a touch of magic to the park, especially in the evening when the illuminated clock resonated the passing hours.*

NYC
LANDMARK

METROPOLITAN
LIFE INSURANCE
TOWER

9 MADISON AVENUE

JUNE 13
1989

THE METROPOLITAN TOWER
ON A SUMMER EVENING

In 1908 the *New York Herald* installed a giant searchlight among the girders at the top of the then-incomplete tower to signal the election results. A northward-swinging beam indicated a majority for Republican William Howard Taft, and a southward beam for Democrat William Jennings Bryan. The beam soon held steady in the northward direction. The results could be seen for miles.

Between 1909 and 1911, Dr. Lee Forrest, the inventor of the radio station, maintained his headquarters atop the home office. Although he occupied this space for only two years, his work in the tower made transatlantic radio communication possible. In 1912 Theodore Roosevelt rose to even greater heights on the very site where he had been baptized (Parkhurst Church), for it was in the tower that his campaign headquarters was located. For nearly seventeen years, the towers of Met Life and Stanford White's Garden stood in harmonious relation to one another when viewed from the park, making Madison Square a major attraction of middle Manhattan.

In April 1964, the fifty-story Met Tower — the only surviving part of the original 1909 Napoleon Le Brun building — was remodeled. Its facade had much of its Tuckahoe marble ornamentation removed and replaced by limestone to make a more harmonious statement with its newly completed adjoining structure. The architects were Lloyd Morgan and Eugene Merone; the contractors were Starrett Brothers and Ehen. On October 31, 1980, the top of the tower (floors 35 to 48) was illuminated on a nightly basis between the hours of nine and midnight. Like the Empire State Building, it is lit in an array of colors for various holidays.

On the practical side, the *Real Estate Record and Guide* pointed out that a single large company building a tower for office purposes ensures itself many advantages. Surrounded by its lower buildings, it preserves light and air that could be so easily blocked by other higher buildings. So, many skyscrapers are designed somewhat as towers but prove not to be architecturally complete as towers due to the fact that the rear and sides of these buildings may someday be hidden by adjoining structures. For Met Life, light and air were even more enhanced by its frontage on the park.

THE EARLY DEMISE OF WHITE'S NEW PARKHURST CHURCH

The next acquisition (phase 9) some ten years later in 1916, brought about the demolition of Stanford White's Madison Square Church. Mr. Frederick Ecker, still the comptroller and responsible for making the church's first move so enticing, once again created another offer and struck a deal with the church. The church was once again uprooted to make room for the ninth addition to Met Life. The demolition of the Madison Square Presbyterian Church met with public outcry and great opposition. In 1919 John J. Chapman wrote in *Vanity Fair*:

The demolition of the Presbyterian Church on Madison Square makes one feel as if our very monuments and triumphal arches were merely the decorations of a parade, or a scaffolding dressed in holiday. Lath and plaster they were, and to lath and plaster they return. There is no room in America for a pastóno, not for a yesterday. This particular church was one of the most careful pieces of work in the city. It was like a Byzantine jewel, so concentrated, well-built and polished, so correct, ornate and lavish that a clever Empress might have had it built. It represented wealth and genius and was one of the few buildings left by Stanford White in which every stone had been weighed, every effect unified. It was brilliant yet solid. It was a little princess of a building, and it did not, as Stanford White's work was apt to do, greet you charmingly and bid you pass on. It brought you to a full stop of admiration.

ABOUT THE MET LIFE CLOCK

- 4 clock faces, each 26½' in diameter, span floors 25–27.

- Minute hands are 17' each weighing 1,000 pounds.

- Hour hands are 13'4" each weighing 700 pounds.

- Numerals are 4' high.

- Round minute marks are 1' in diameter.

- Each face runs on 1/24 horsepower motor.

- Time is reset with crank, mechanisms for all four clocks controlled by a master clock in the basement.

- Four chimes located on 46th floor, higher than any other chimes in the world when installed.

- Chimes sound a measure from Handel's "I Know That My Redeemer Liveth," also referred to as "Cambridge Quarters."

- The bells were cast in 1908 by Meneely Bell Co., Troy, New York.

- The largest bell is B flat at 7,000 pounds, followed by E flat at 3,000 pounds, F at 2,000 pounds, and G at 1,500 pounds.

- The acoustics in the campanile are such that the chimes can be heard for miles, while workers in the floors directly below go about their normal business undisturbed.

- The chimes sound between 8 A.M. and 10 P.M. After 10 P.M. the tower light flashes red on the quarter hour and white on the hour.

- The octagonal lantern, "the light that never fails," atop the tower is 8' in diameter. People as far away as Sandy Hook, New Jersey, can set their watches to the flashing light on a clear night.

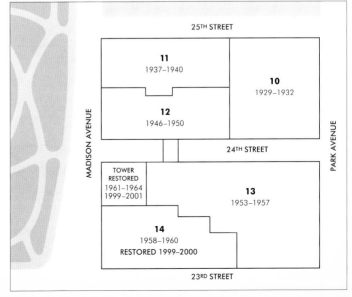

... The Americans change buildings every few years as one changes cars in traveling. Hawthorne said that the American would no more think of using his father's house than of wearing his father's coat. The pressure of space in our cities has left no corner for anything except for the trick-buildings and extravaganzas of commerce. The very merits of these office-buildings and apartments are a ghastly comment on the age. They emphasize our detachment from the past by the very links into which they bind us to the past. ... Good architecture is the mightiest artistic power in the world. It passes on the shadow of humanity from one age to the next as no other art can do. It speaks to the mind of the infant without the need of an interpreter. It does not merely hark back to the past. Any great building is the past — an enduring unescapable, present reality. It creates literature, feeding the world with ever more imagination, and growing more potent in its decay than it was in its prime.

An anonymous writer of *The Nation*'s "In the Driftwood" wrote, "'Twas all on account of the Madison Square Church. That had been Stanford White's masterpiece. ... It carried Rome and the Renaissance on toward the ultimates. It took five thousand years to achieve that church ... and they demolished it in a week."

130 *During the 1920s, Madison Avenue between 24th and 25th Streets was occupied by Met Life and three other office buildings. Ample parking was available in the middle of Fifth Avenue and Broadway.*

131 *Diagram B— Showing the building program for the Metropolitan Life from 1929 to present.*

THE CONTINUING EXPANSION OF MET LIFE

Ten years passed. As the need for more space continued, the company planned quite a monumental undertaking (phases 10, 11, 12). The north building, between 24th and 25th Streets, was designed by the firm of Wald, Corbett and Angilly that had worked on Radio City. A *New York Times* article said of this new towering addition: "The building is not fashioned after some predetermined architectural style, but is essentially a creation of this age and time." In other words, it answered several given problems. First, that Met Life was to be the sole tenant. Second, that all the service lines were to be located in a central core, allowing for more floor space. And finally, the actual shape of the building would be determined by the city's zoning laws. Corbett further reiterated that "at last architects have arrived at the point of view

that considers first the purpose of which a building is erected and then determines, through arrangement of the various elements of the design, the pleasing relationships and balances that are, and have always been, the prime factors in the designs of all enduring architecture."

Cass Gilbert, who had completed the New York Life Insurance building just one year prior in 1928, had to work within the same prescribed zoning laws which allowed buildings to rise to greater heights on broader streets or avenues than on narrow ones. If a building had unlimited height, this would reduce the number of hours of sunlight illuminating the street. Therefore the law stated that buildings could rise to a height one and a half the width of the street before it would have to be set back. There is then a further formula to determine setbacks on higher floors.

132 *The second phase of the north building of Metropolitan Life under construction in the late 1930s. The first phase had been completed and that part of the building was fully occupied and functioning independently.*

133 *The original plan for this building, which was published in the* New York Times *on November 3, 1929, pictured a building of one hundred stories. The design, reminiscent of an out-of-control Tower of Babel, must have caused quite a stir. It took only two weeks for the plans to be revised to its current height of thirty-one stories. Certainly one of the reasons for curtailing its proposed height was that it would have dwarfed the company's very own tower, which had evolved into their corporate symbol.*

The building schedule and plan were quite ingenious, for what appears to be one colossal building was built in three very separate stages from 1929 to 1950. Upon completion of each third of the building, employees moved in and offices went into full operation. The Art Deco–style structure, with its wedding-cake-like setbacks, was faced with Alabama limestone.

10– The first part of this complex, covering Fourth Avenue between 24th and 25th Streets, was started in 1929 and rose twenty-eight stories above and four stories below street level, creating twenty-two acres of additional office space.

11– Met Life acquired the two corner office buildings, which up to this point had been privately owned. This second unit, built between 1937 and 1940, completed the 25th Street facade and extended to within a few feet of the annex buildings. Its twenty-eight stories were slightly more then half the size of the first unit.

12– The final unit of this complex was erected between 1946 and 1950 and replaced the Met Annex Building, which had been erected in 1916, replacing the second Parkhurst Church. There are four enormous vaulted exterior vestibules located at the corners of this mammoth building. These entrances, at the corners of Madison and Park Avenues and 24th and 25th Streets, were designed to be secured each night by moving a monumental four-part gate into place. These decorative and functional closures were designed and fabricated by Rambusch in the early 1930s and were installed as each phase of construction was completed. The plantlike forms that graced each gate were cast in monel, a non-corrosive alloy of nickel and copper, a material that retains its silvery appearance and was popular during the Art Deco period.

13– Between 1953 and 1957 a new structure was erected, taking the place of several original buildings (numbers 2, 4, 5, and 7 on diagram A).

14– The entire two-block complex was completed in 1960, with a new building of clean-cut limestone replacing the very first twelve-story Renaissance-style structure. Rambusch was once again called upon to perform in another area of its expertise. This time the company was asked to disassemble the original board room, an elaborate inner chamber with tooled-leather walls, deeply carved mahogany paneling, marble fireplaces and a richly decorated ceiling. It was totally cleaned, the wood was waxed, the tooled leather reconditioned and the ceiling re-gilded with 23-karat gold leaf. To enhance the light given by period fixtures, recessed lighting was installed in the room's new location.

Upon its seventy-fifth anniversary, an issue of *Home Office* said of its surroundings on the park, "The Home Office Buildings of the company, facing a city park, have the advantage of an admirable location. The approach from the west emphasizes this preeminence. The stateliness of the Tower and the impressive dignity of the entire group are further enhanced by the foreground of foliage. Few businesses are blessed with such a setting."

CREDIT SUISSE FIRST BOSTON

In 1996 the financial institution of Credit Suisse First Boston moved to Madison Square, leasing the giant north building from the Metropolitan Life Insurance Company. With the need for one million square feet of office space, CS First Boston found the Metropolitan Life Building perfectly suited. For a year, scaffolding surrounded the building while portions of it were totally gutted and altered for the new company. Met Life had vacated the building after sixty-six years to move this portion of its operations to a new home, the former Pan Am Building at 42nd Street. Located in the middle of Park Avenue, adjacent to Grand Central Station, here the company would be able to once again insure its longevity of uninterrupted light and high visibility. As of this writing, CS had announced plans to take over all but the eleventh floor of 1 Madison Avenue and also occupy several floors in the Met Life Tower, leaving approximately 500 Met Life associates of the original 24,000 employees that filled this complex at one time.

In 1999 a total restoration commenced on the tower, followed in 2000 by work on number One Madison Avenue. Building Conservation Associates, Inc., was in charge of the restoration work, which included removal of decades worth of accumulated soiling from the exterior stone facades, a masonry repair and replacement program addressing 7,000 conditions on the tower alone, restoration of the four monumental clock faces, and gilding the cupola with 23.75-karat Italian gold leaf.

A RETURN TO ELEGANT DINING

Credit Suisse First Boston leased the impressive ground floor along Madison Avenue opposite the park to Danny Meyer, the noted restaurant impresario, for two of his dining establishments — Tabla at 25th Street and Eleven Madison at 24th Street. There had not been an elegant dining spot on the park since Delmonico's occupied the southwest corner of 26th Street and Fifth Avenue. The difference between the arrival of these two restaurateurs on the park was that when Charles Delmonico moved here in 1876, Madison Square sparkled with newly laid out and freshly planted paths designed by Ignatz Pilat. One hundred and thirty years had taken their toll, and Danny Meyer had his work cut out. He became instrumental in the revitalization and restoration of Madison Square Park.

134 *The completed Metropolitan Life complex in the late 1950s.*

5

MADISON SQUARE SOUTH

A BLOCK IN TRANSITION

Even though 23rd Street between Broadway and Madison Avenue today is visually the least appealing stretch of avenue to border Madison Square, it is probably the most interesting when it comes to preservation. Here are the remnants of two brownstone structures from the 1800s that have survived into the twenty-first century: number 20 East 23rd Street — the most intact building, missing only its front steps that would have led to the parlor — and number 14, with its ground floor appearing much like any other commercial structure, while its third and fourth floors retain the character of the original brownstone structure. Number 14 clearly illustrates the transition of this block from residential to commercial.

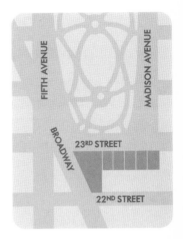

DANIEL F. TIEMANN

In 1832 the Tiemann family bought ten acres of land at 23rd Street between Broadway and Fourth Avenue, upon which they built a two-and-a-half-story frame house. It was located near their family-owned paint factory. The land had been part of the farmland of John Watt. Daniel Tiemann lived here until September 1839, when, at the age of thirty-four, he moved to Manhattanville, where he represented the Sixteenth Ward in the Common Council for two years. His mother and father lived in this house for the rest of their lives. In 1851 he was elected Alderman of the Twelfth Ward, and then in 1853 was elected to a five-year term on the Board of Governors of Charities and Correction; in the fourth year of that term, friends and supporters urged him to run for mayor. The fight was against Fernando Wood and Tammany Hall methods of politics. Wood, a Democrat, had served as mayor from 1855 to 1857.

OPPOSITE

135 *Looking east along 23rd Street from the point at which Fifth Avenue crosses Broadway. The building at the corner of 23rd Street and Broadway housed the Louvre, considered to be one of the upscale concert saloons of its time. Adjacent, to the east, was the photo studio of William Kurtz, followed by a line of brownstone row houses that reached to Madison Avenue, defining the southern boundary of Madison Square.*

136 *The home of Daniel Tiemann, on East 23rd Street opposite the southeastern end of the park. Seen in the background is the old Calvary Church at 21st Street and Fourth Avenue.*

Wood was an unscrupulous character who accepted graft payments from Robert Lowber, a Wall Street broker who had amassed a fortune for himself by selling land to the city at exorbitant prices. Upon taking office in 1858, Tiemann, who ran as an independent, was determined to reform the administration and refused to pay Lowber $169,000 for a parcel of land worth $60,000, a deal instigated by former Mayor Wood. The broker sued and won, demanding not only his $169,000 but also interest charges and legal fees, for a total of $228,000. When the city comptroller said that there were no funds available, the matter was turned over to the sheriff, who, under law, had to obey the court's decision. His solution was to auction off City Hall and its contents, including the mayor's chair. Rumor began to circulate that Wood, the very wealthy ex-mayor, would be present at the sale and purchase City Hall, and then in turn offer the use of the building to city officials. Tiemann, outraged by the thought, placed a bid through a clerk for $50,000. The outcome was that Wood never appeared and Tiemann won the bid, making him, for one brief moment, the sole owner of City Hall. It was soon bought back from him at the price he paid, and the Wall Street broker was reimbursed, ending the matter. During Tiemann's administration, Wood abandoned Tammany Hall, organized his own independent Democratic organization, and won the race for mayor in 1859.

One of Tiemann's first public acts was to stop the sale of liquor in City Hall. He also originated the custom of placing street names on city street lamps.

THE MYSTERIOUS COLGATE HOUSE

The homes along the south side of Madison Square Park, at first a continuous row of brownstones and home to several prominent families, were some of the first structures to be converted for commercial use. Several were uprooted to make way for the first small commercial buildings on the park.

Opposite the southeast corner of the park, at number 22 East 23rd Street, was the home of Robert Colgate, founder of the notable soap firm. The unique location where Madison Avenue begins afforded the family an uninterrupted view up the Avenue as well as a prestigious place on the park. He and his family lived here until 1918, when they suddenly abandoned their home on the square. In 1944 Miss Jessie Colgate Colby, the family's sole descendant, decided to sell the house and land that the Colgates and Colbys had owned since 1831 to the Ren-West Realty Company; it was to be torn down to make way for a one-story taxpayer. For twenty-seven years the house and its contents had stood untouched, visited only on occasion by a guard to check the burglar alarm. Upon its sale, boards were removed from its entrance and its French windows were opened wide. Miss Jessie Colby's cousin, Mrs. Susan Colgate Cleveland, of New London, New Hampshire, had come to sort out the extraordinary furnishings and personal belongings, an impressive accumulation of a century or more. Thousands of people on the street who passed this house stopped to gape at the ancient brownstone front that had once been one of the finest homes on Madison Square. Lou Baum, a retired actor from Brooklyn and self-appointed guide of this historic event, answered questions of the curious with authority. A merchant from the Flatiron Building offered to pay admission to get a glimpse of the inside. From out of the crowd came an elderly gentleman by the name of H. F. LaFlamme, who went right up to the front door and rang the bell; there was no response. He told the crowd, "I was an old friend of the late James C. Colgate. . . . Many's the time I've walked by here with Mr. Colgate when he talked of the happy evenings he'd spent in this

house." The crowds peered through the dusty parlor windows at the elegant objects of a Victorian past, covered with at least six inches of dust. There were gold chandeliers, marble columns, elaborately carved gilt-framed mirrors, paintings and mahogany furniture. Unlike Mr. LaFlamme, museum experts and appraisers were cautiously admitted by Pete Morgan of Morgan and Brothers movers. His packers, Walter Roth and John O'Day, emerged from time to time covered in black. Dealers with their educated eye had no trouble seeing through the layers of years. A dealer spotting a blue-and-white vessel on the marble mantel identified it as an Egyptian Gendeameri vase. He offered $500 for it. He also noted that the gilt frames were real gold leaf because they had remained so bright. The silver, however, had turned black and the closets stood filled with clothes. Mrs. Cleveland had to call in a locksmith to open a French wardrobe whose key, of course, was nowhere to be found. Onlookers were able to catch a glimpse of the museum-quality objects as they were removed. The house sold for far less than its assessed value of $77,000. Before James Colby, a cousin, died, he had refused a $100,000 offer. The site of the Colgate residence today is home, in a way, to another corporate giant, McDonalds.

Number 26 was the home of the adventurous entrepreneur Amos Eno, who had moved his family from Washington Square Park in 1856 so that he could closely follow the progress of the construction of the Fifth Avenue Hotel.

APERTURE

Since 1982 the sole surviving nineteenth-century brownstone, at number 20 East 23rd Street on Madison Square and at the foot of Madison Avenue, has been home to Aperture, a photographic foundation concerned with the innovation, exhibition and reproduction of fine photography. (Prior to their appearance on the park, this structure was home to the offices of Woodlawn Cemetery; their grounds, located since 1863 in the wooded beauty of the Bronx River Valley, are the final resting place for many of Madison Square's prestigious families. Also interred there are the remains of Admiral David Farragut.) Aperture holds gallery exhibitions in the Burden Gallery, located on the ground floor. The second floor is used for further exhibition space and gallery talks. These rooms retain much of their original architectural detail and decorative moldings and have a wonderful view overlooking the park and an endless view up Madison Avenue.

137 *From left to right, numbers 24, 22, and 20 East 23rd Street, facing Madison Square Park. Number 22 shows the abandoned and overgrown Colgate house. To the right, the former offices of Woodlawn Cemetery and today home to Aperture, a well-known photography foundation, bookstore and gallery.*

138 *Number 20 today, altered for commercial use and home to Aperture, clearly maintains some of its original architectural features from the late 1800s. Even without its Italiante detailing, its cornice and windows suggest the scale and type of homes that once surrounded Madison Square.*

It is in this generous space that Aperture has been able to interact directly with the public and to bring original works by some of photography's masters and also little-known artists to a new and important audience. It was the dream of Shirley Carter Burden, the foundation's chairman until his death in 1989, to create an exhibition space free of the marketplace demands of the gallery system. Just as William Kurtz, a resident photographer at number 6 East 23rd, used his exhibition space to feature works of experimentation and innovation, Burden intended his gallery to be used as a laboratory where new ideas and creative expressions were to be encouraged.

The inspiration for Aperture dates back to the early twentieth century, to Alfred Stieglitz's famed "laboratory centers" and his influential but short-lived publication, Camera Work. It was through Stieglitz's periodical, his gallery shows at 291 Fifth Avenue, and his association with Edward Steichen and Paul Strand, that masterworks of an extraordinary generation of European and American photographers were able to reach a public audience.

In the fifties, a small group of photographers — Ansel Adams, Dorothea Lange, Barbara Morgan, and Minor White — together with historian Beaumont Newhall and writer Nancy Newhall, created Aperture, a quarterly photographic periodical. Its creators stated: "Aperture has been originated to communicate with serious photographers and creative people everywhere, whether professional, amateur, or student. . . . We, who have founded this Journal, invite others to use Aperture as a common ground for the advancement of photography."

Minor White was the editor of Aperture, and in the mid-sixties, he was joined by a former student, Michael E. Hoffman, who today continues as the foundation's executive director. Hoffman assumed most of the editing and publishing duties and was also responsible for creating Aperture's book-publishing program that included the monographs of well-known photographers. Publications have also been created to accompany exhibitions arranged in collaboration with major art museums.

In the mid-seventies, Paul Strand created the Paul Strand Foundation, which became part of Aperture. From it the Paul Strand Archive emerged, attracting contributions from outstanding photographers and making it a unique resource for artists and scholars.

THE BROOKS FAMILY

In 1851 Edward Sands Brooks built a brownstone at number 18. His grandfather, Dr. David Brooks, a physician from Connecticut, moved to New York in 1747 and took up residence at the northwest corner of Catherine and Cherry Streets. In 1818 his son Henry Sands Brooks opened the original men's clothing store on the site of his father's home, where it remained until 1874. Henry's son Edward entered the business in 1845 and, along with his brothers Daniel H., John, and Elisha, opened a second store at Broadway and Grand Street in 1857, where they remained until 1870. During the Civil War, Brooks Brothers was enlisted to produce uniforms for Generals Grant, Sherman, Sheridan, and Hood as well as thousands of troops. (Tiffany's turned out swords, medals, corps badges, and military insignia.) Between 1870 and 1884, Edward saw the store move to two other locations, Union Square South and Bond Street. Edward died while the store was on Bond Street, and Daniel H. Brooks, the last of his surviving sons, retired from the business in 1879, at

A GRANDSON REMEMBERS

Edward Brooks' grandson, William Owen, recalls in a memoir he wrote in 1938 about the view from his grandfather's home on Madison Square South in the early 1850s:

At that time there was a picket fence around the square, or "Park" as we used to call it, and Corporal Thompson's Cottage still stood at the northwest corner of Fifth Avenue and Twenty-third Street. To the north there was to be seen little more than a vast extent of vacant lots, broken only by the Reservoir at Fifth Avenue and 42nd Street, which looked like a distant fortress.

He further recounts that the Hippodrome, which replaced Corporal Thompson's Madison Cottage, was destroyed by fire and was soon replaced by the Fifth Avenue Hotel. Owen recalls his boyhood visits to the nearby hotel, where he would sit in the famed "amen corner," just to say that he had sat there. From the hotel's windows he watched the passing Decoration Day parades, attended by the president of the United States. He remembers Grover Cleveland at one such celebration in 1885. In the hotel he also spotted General Benjamin F. Butler in military garb. The day before Lincoln's reelection, in 1863, Butler had been sent to New York City with almost 10,000 troops to guard against confederate threats to burn down the city. Edward recognized him from the Eden Musee, a popular house of entertainment located a few doors west of the hotel on 23rd Street, where Butler was one of the many figures portrayed in which time several of the employees became associated partners. Brooks Brothers moved to Broadway and 22nd Street, just one block south of Madison Square Park, in 1884, the year the Brooklyn Bridge opened. They remained at this location for thirty-one years, until they finally settled at Madison Avenue and 44th Street in 1915.

139 *The former home of the Brooks family altered for the Scott Stamp and Coin Company.*

THE SCOTT STAMP AND COIN COMPANY

One of the earliest commercial ventures on 23rd Street was the Scott Stamp and Coin Company, which came to occupy what had been the parlor floor of the Brooks family brownstone. The business was established by John W. Scott in 1863. He was the first person to devote himself solely to the stamp-collecting business. Before long his interests grew to include coin collecting as well. In 1868 he produced the first stamp album and periodical, followed by numerous journals and catalogs on the subject. *The American Journal of Philately,* the quintessential stamp-collecting publication, and the *Catalogue for Advanced Collectors* were two of the publications he produced.

It was here on Madison Square that Scott housed his vast treasure of stamp and coin history, including specimens issued by every nation. Stamp and coin enthusiasts came here from far and wide to see and purchase Scott's rare finds as well as items necessary for their hobbies, such as the "International Stamp Album," with a capacity to hold 15,000 varieties of stamps, and equivalent receptacles for their coins. Scott sold the company in 1885 and retired from business. The Scott Publishing Company today is located in Sidney, Ohio. This 23rd Street site is occupied today by a five-story commercial structure.

wax. He also remembered seeing movies" for the first time at the den. The subjects of these short akes were of everyday city life: a ire engine racing by, a river with a teamboat gliding by, and men and women crossing a street under the supervision of a policeman.

Other of Owen's recollections were of some of the local characters identified with the Madison Square neighborhood: an old hunch-acked bootblack known as Quilp," a Dickens character who pointed at men's shoes in silence and grinned idiotically, a blind man who sat on a one-legged stool and played the accordion, and the two policemen stationed at the long crossing" (one at Fifth Avenue and 23rd Street, the other at Broadway and 23rd Street; one was nicknamed "Dignity," the other Impudence" for his intimate, sometimes off-color remarks to people). Another memory of Owen's childhood was the strong presence of Catherine Lorillard Wolfe, whose gracious home stood at the northeast corner of Madison Avenue and 24th Street. This distinctive brownstone was three stories high and three windows wide, with the front door between the two parlor windows facing the park. He remembers her on one occasion standing at her window waving a handkerchief and smiling at the joyful salutations of a long line of boys and girls from some institution marching by her house two by two. She was sending them for a splendid afternoon to Barnum and Bailey's "Greatest Show on Earth" performance at Madison Square Garden, only two short blocks up the Avenue.

THE MENLO PARK CERAMIC WORKS

In 1888, at number 16 East 23rd Street, one of the first commercial loft buildings on the square was erected by Jer. T. Smith for the offices and warehouse of his Menlo Park Ceramic Works. The manufacturing company itself was located in Menlo Park, New Jersey. Smith produced tiling, wainscoting and faience mantels in various colorings. Smith was a leading builder and contractor, much sought after by the city's leading architects. For example, he worked on the Metropolitan Life Building, located directly across from his new offices on 23rd Street. On this project alone he utilized approximately 90,000 square feet of materials produced by his company. Numbers 10 and 12 East 23rd have exact facades as number 16.

140 *The Menlo Park Ceramic Works, at number 16, is identical to the two six-story buildings that fill a double lot two doors away.*

THE KURTZ PHOTOGRAPHIC STUDIO

At number 6 East 23rd Street, William Kurtz, an innovator in the photomechanical process, had set up his impressive photo studio and gallery and, in time, rented space to the American Art Galleries, which would evolve into the auction house of Sotheby's Parke-Bernet.

Kurtz was born in Germany in 1834. He went to London and became a lithographer and drawing teacher, and then as a result of a ship journey gone awry, he found himself in New York in 1859. Here he obtained a job as an artist who "finished" the prints of the early collodion negatives in crayon and oil. Collodion was a thick, syrupy liquid made by dissolving nitrated cotton in a mixture of alcohol and ether. It served as a vehicle to hold the light-sensitive material to the glass plate. In 1865 he opened a photographic gallery at 872 Broadway, followed in 1874 by his better-known gallery on Madison Square Park for the exhibition of photographs and art reproductions. On the facade of the building was a large female figure holding a lens, an ornamental sculpture by George Hess.

The photographic career of Kurtz coincided with the introduction of the cabinet photograph in 1866. This new larger-format photograph measuring 4 x 5½ inches gave photographers an opportunity to work with posing and lighting their subjects more artfully than the popular carte-de-visite,

141 *The enterprising and talented William Kurtz, whose innovations and experimentation in photography had a direct influence on the development of four-color printing.*

OPPOSITE

142 *The back of a Kurtz cabinet photograph that bore his elaborate logo. It included the words "Paris, Vienna, Philadelphia, and New York," three renderings of medals he had received in recognition of his work, and a central swirling banner with "W. Kurtz, New York, Madison Square."*

which had been introduced in 1859. These smaller 2½ x 4-inch portraits produced from an untouched negative and printed directly on albumen paper were in great demand until 1865. For the first time, one was able to see multiple images of oneself, usually in full length, and the relatively inexpensive costs of twenty-five copies for a dollar made these most attractive to the masses, who could enclose photos in letters to distant friends and relatives.

Greater skill was now needed in the mechanics of the cabinet photograph because the flaws that were not obvious in the small cards now became conspicuous. The practice of retouching the negatives was adapted to remove wrinkles and facial blemishes, smooth hair, and create a greater variety of intermediate tones. The early formal art training of Kurtz was a definite asset for him with the introduction of the larger format. It was this experience that helped him in the development and perfecting of the "Rembrandt" photograph.

143 *The distinctive building that Kurtz designed took full advantage of his location on the park. The upper floors featured a glass bay window and skylit rooms to utilize every bit of available light. He cared greatly about his image on the park and elaborately adorned his building for public holidays and celebrations (see page 127).*

Unlike those who were dependent on retouching negatives to achieve a certain effect, his art was in the lighting of his subject. He did this in such a way that the effect produced was like that of the light-and-shade method perfected by the Dutch artist Rembrandt. Before his innovation, most portrait photography was achieved by simply turning the subject's face toward the light. Because of the slow speed of the collodion negative, which was not capable of registering any great range of light intensities, the subject had to be well lit, or over-lit, to reduce the long exposure needed. This resulted in a loss of modeling in the face and produced a flat and uninteresting photograph. The

Rembrandt portrait was beyond the ability of most photographers, who did not have the artistic eye of Kurtz or his formal art training. In other words, Kurtz knew when and when not to use this effect, whereas many photographers misused the method.

Kurtz was one of several noted portrait photographers who worked closely with Moses King, publisher of a series of late-nineteenth-century books on New York City. One of these most ambitious books was *Notable New Yorkers,* which documented the images of most of the city's well-known citizens.

Kurtz went on to become interested in the reproduction of magazine and book illustrations in color. Color illustrations were possible by using three-color halftone cuts — red, yellow and blue — and were being used as early as 1885. Some of Kurtz's experiments in color were reproductions of birds in which he tried to capture the brilliant plumage of his stuffed subjects. One of the first books to be published at a popular price that exhibited the technique and utilized his experimental plates was a work by Neltje Blatchan entitled *Bird Neighbors.* Kurtz invested a great deal of money and time in perfecting his new process that would become the basis of four-color printing widely prevalent today. He died before he was able to witness its great commercial success.

An innovator in the business of photography, Kurtz spared no expense in his flamboyant style, as seen in the unusual building on Madison Square and his effort at self-promotion. The back of each one of his cabinet photos bore his elaborate logo. He won both local and international recognition for his work, including his Rembrandt photo process. At the American Institute's annual fair in 1870, he was awarded first prize for "the best plain photography, the best photograph finish in Indian Ink and the best photograph on porcelain." He was also awarded the first prize for "the best crayon drawings," recognizing his true artistic abilities. In 1871 he was the only American awarded a medal at the International Photographic Exhibition held in Vienna, where he received one of the two most prestigious awards for portrait photographers, the other going to Loescher and Petsch of Berlin.

THE AMERICAN ART ASSOCIATION

On the top floor of the Kurtz Studios building, exhibitions and sales of the American Art Association were held. The formative years of Sotheby Park-Bernet began and continued here on Madison Square until 1922. Anson Phelps Stokes, the chief chronicler of New York, noted:

The American Art Association was formed in the early 1870s by James F. Stanton, R. Austin Robertson, and Thomas E. Kirby, for the encouragement and promotion of American Art. . . . It possessed the lease of The American Art Gallery, consisting of a room 46' x 36', with adjoining offices, in the building of

REMBRANDT EFFECT

In his book *Photography and the American Scene,* Robert Taft relates that Kurtz explained his method in the following way:

When in the dark-room preparing plates, I often see my subjects assume very graceful positions, which it seems almost impossible to get myself when I go to pose them. Therefore, when they come in I seat them on this platform and watch them from the darkroom. When they assume a post I like, I step out, ask them to keep it, and I wheel them under the light where I want them.

Subjects were now positioned under a series of screens and top and side-lights that could be quickly altered. Either a plain background was used or the subject was actually placed against the light, which, with the aid of the side-lights, relieved "the dark parts of the sitter on a light background and the lighter part of the sitter on a darker background." Kurtz's most innovative device was the counter reflector, a movable two-wing construction covered with tin-foil, used to fill in the shadow side, thus creating the subtle modeling that was characteristic of the Rembrandt photograph.

Wm. Kurtz, a photographer, at 6–8 East Twenty-Third Street. . . . The business of the Association is the exhibition and sale of works of art and literature.

Thomas E. Kirby, an ambitious and imaginative young auctioneer, was responsible for the success of this new organization. The association originally dealt exclusively with exhibitions and retail sales, but in 1885, as a result of an economic downturn, New York's Metropolitan Bank failed and had to liquidate its extensive art collection. Kirby persuaded his partners to undertake the bank's sale "in a manner befitting the aims and ideals of their organization . . . by managing the auction as an important artistic, cultural, and social event." He instituted imposing receptions with a "distinctly society flavor." The sale was a grand success, including the exhibition, catalogue, publicity and auction, placing the American Art Association in a league removed from the shoddy image of many of the auctioneers of the time.

In 1886 James Fountain Sutton, son-in-law of Rowland H. Macy, a colleague of Robertson, mounted the first French Impressionist show in America. They arranged to have the famous art dealer Paul Durand-Ruel send over 289 works of art, including oils by Renoir, Manet, Degas, and Pissarro. This show on Madison Square was well received by its New York audience.

The ground floor of the Kurtz Building was home for many years to the famous Dorlon's restaurant, where those who shopped the "Ladies Mile" (the shopping district located between 14th and 23rd Streets and Broadway and Sixth Avenue) might stop and think of having chicken patties, the specialty of the house. Apparently oysters were another, since bold letters encircling the dial of a sidewalk clock that stood at its entrance, along with four ornamental gas lamps, indicated that this location was the "Oyster Branch."

THE BIRTH OF PARKE-BERNET

"The American Art Association prospered and collectors and dealers benefited from the high standards, informative catalogues, and attractively arranged pre-sale exhibitions that became synonymous with the firm." Major art auctions were held at Chickering Hall, at Fifth Avenue and

18th Street, Mendelssohn Hall, at Broadway and 40th Street, and eventually at the Plaza Hotel on Fifth Avenue, with other sales held at their original Madison Square location. It was here, November 25–27, 1907, that many objects that had been owned by Stanford White were auctioned just one year after his death. They were items he had acquired for use in the construction and interior embellishments of future mansions and other buildings.

The association moved in 1922 from 23rd Street to Madison Avenue and 57th Street. During the first forty years, some $60 million worth of art and antiques, jewels and rare books had been sold to an ever-growing audience of dealers and collectors, and the foundation had been laid for the future course of the American Art Association and its successors.

Cortlandt Field Bishop, a known collector, became the new owner of the American Art Association, and along with Hiram Parke and Otto Bernet, they continued in the tradition that Kirby had established. The most notable competition in this field was Anderson Galleries, which the American Art Association bought in 1929, formally merging the two. The new gallery was named American Art Association–Anderson Galleries, Inc.

It was in 1937, when Bishop's widow threatened to bring Kennerly, the genius behind the Anderson Galleries, out of retirement that Parke, Bernet, and their staff formed a new company, Parke-Bernet. Their first auction was held at a temporary gallery space at 742 Fifth Avenue in the Bergdorf Goodman Building, and they soon relocated to their new home at 30 East 57th Street, and then moved again to a more residential neighborhood at 980 Madison Avenue.

In 1955 Sotheby's, the London-based auction house, opened a New York office, and in 1964 Sotheby's acquired Parke-Bernet, which, by this time, was the largest fine-art auction house in the United States.

THE LOUVRE AND THE BARTHOLDI HOTEL

On the southwest corner of Broadway and 23rd Streets in the mid- to late-1800s, the Louvre, one of the more famous upscale and classy concert saloons, was located. There were more than three hundred of these establishments in operation at the time, although it was reported by Police Commissioner John A. Kennedy that seventy-five were of ill repute. These houses employed "the prettiest waiter girls found in the world, maintaining agents in all parts of the United States, England, and France, to engage the most accomplished ladies." Admission for gentlemen was usually twenty-five cents; ladies were admitted free. The spacious rooms of the Louvre, overlooking the park, included a drinking room with an ornate mirrored bar and a sparkling fountain, a billiard parlor, and a smaller, quieter lounge where only champagne was served. It was one of New York's most exciting sites with its glittering crystal chandeliers, marble columns, and walls paneled in gold and emerald and frescoed with baskets of fruits and bouquets of flowers. Light musical entertainment was offered, and the audience was encouraged to interact with the performers by joining in on the chorus and socializing with them between acts. The waiter girls, who typically wore low-cut bodices and very short skirts, accentuating bare legs with high tasseled red boots, were not servants but companions. At the Louvre, it was said that "one who found oneself in a transient or disconnected state could cultivate the art of real happiness." The waiter girls were known to approach a gentleman and take his order, then sit down and join him in a drink. Sexual encounters could be arranged on the premises or at nearby brothels. At some of the lower-class saloons, the patrons were known to be beaten and robbed and their drinks drugged. Most of the waiter girls were drawn to this vocation by lack of employment, and many were supporting aged mothers and paying to educate younger brothers and sisters. The Louvre was in proximity to the Madison Square Presbyterian Church, but was gone by the time Reverend Parkhurst took his stand against such houses.

The Louvre was replaced by the Bartholdi Hotel, named after the sculptor of the Statue of Liberty, Frédéric-Auguste Bartholdi. The arm of the statue had stood in Madison Square Park within easy view of this popular location from 1876 to 1884.

This structure occupied this corner site until October 17, 1966, when a tragic fire broke out in an art-supply store at 7 East 22nd Street. The fire spread rapidly through an adjoining drugstore and north along Broadway towards the corner building on 23rd Street. Twelve firemen entered the drugstore, knocking out the back wall in an effort to reach the fire. Suddenly a 100-square-foot section of floor collapsed, triggering a firestorm. All twelve firemen perished instantly. The buildings had housed many artists' and photographers' lofts and studios. The lifework of well-known photographer Gjon Mili was all but totally destroyed. While the fire still raged, *Life* magazine sent a crew to try to rescue whatever images they could from wooden filing cabinets stored along the eastern wall of his studio, which was the last to burn. The destruction resulted in the entire block between 22nd and 23rd Streets along Broadway being leveled and turned into a parking lot.

In 1975 a proposal was made for an apartment complex to be built upon the site, and in 1983 the plan was realized. Madison Green, designed by Phillip Birnbaum, rose on the vacant lot, and on its 23rd Street facade a plaque was mounted in memory of the twelve firefighters who gave their lives in this tragedy.

146a *The Bartholdi Hotel, at the corner of 23rd and Broadway, home today to Madison Green.*

146b *Madison Green.*

MADISON GREEN

The thirty-one-story Madison Green stopped just shy of its immediate neighbor, the twenty-one-story Flatiron Building. The new structure was not allowed to exceed the height of the famous landmark. Ingeniously, ten additional floors were incorporated into the new condominium building, providing the owners more saleable units. Most significant was its impact on the Flatiron Building itself. Madison Green not only obstructed the natural daylight afforded tenants of the famous landmark on the building's east facade but also minimized the Flatiron's majestic presence on the square. It was the grand breadth of Broadway at 23rd Street that saved the Flatiron from being encroached upon further.

6
THE FLATIRON BUILDING

A Triangular Plot at the "Center of the United States"

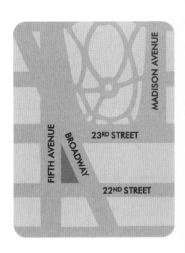

The Flatiron Building was built on the triangular site where Fifth Avenue crosses Broadway at 23rd Street. In 1867 this parcel of land was purchased by Amos Eno, owner of the Fifth Avenue Hotel, and was known as "Eno's Triangle," "Eno's Corner" and the "cowcatcher." Having paid $32,000, he and his heirs collected millions from rentals. The term *cowcatcher*, by which this triangular plot of land was called well before the Flatiron's appearance, could have evolved from the fact that early residents who came to live on Madison Square were known to keep an occasional farm animal on their property. Perhaps a few strays found their way onto this triangular bit of land seeking a safe haven from the growing number of carriages and commercial wagons that tried to negotiate this increasingly busy intersection. This oddly shaped patch of green almost became an extension of Madison Square Park, but the city was reluctant to finance the project since the price was much higher than the accepted valuation. Negative public opinion led to abandoning this plan.

The south end of this triangular lot between Fifth and Broadway at 22nd Street was occupied first by the St. Germaine Hotel, which was to become the Cumberland Apartments. A sign projected by magic lantern onto its north facade proclaimed, "The Center of the United States — Here." Other tenants on the triangle included a photographer, a "painless" dentist, a chiropodist and a shirtmaker. The ticket office for the Erie Railroad and the Wells Fargo Company were located at the point.

OPPOSITE

147 *With the anticipation of the Flatiron Building, newspapers and magazines took it upon themselves to create their own renditions of the finished structure before it was physically complete. Here an artist chose to create a detached circular gazebo where the "cowcatcher," the attached odd protrusion that we see today, was soon to appear.*

148 *A photo from the 1850s looking north on Fifth Avenue from 22nd Street. To the right, the St. Germaine Hotel stands on the southerly portion of the famous triangular plot of land between 22nd and 23rd Streets, with the park and rowhouses along Madison Square North clearly visible in the background.*

Most tenants on this site vacated to make way for the new skyscraper. There was, however, one holdout: Colonel Winfield Scott Roskey, a member of the staff of the governor of Florida. He held out while gas pipes were cut off and stores were demolished. He finally got an injunction and came to terms with the new owners.

GEORGE A. FULLER AND DANIEL H. BURNHAM

The mining fortunes made out West by two wealthy businessmen were actually responsible for the creation of the Flatiron Building. Samuel Newhouse, "the copper king," who had moved from Pennsylvania to Colorado in the 1880s after a brief stint in newspaper work, engaged in freight transportation and later made his fortune in copper. He built the Newhouse Hotel in Salt Lake City, which he claimed to be the first real skyscraper. Newhouse bought the triangular plot of land at 23rd Street in New York City in 1899 from the Eno family for $690,000. Eno had owned this land more than forty years. In 1901 this unique site was sold by Newhouse and his associates to the Fuller Company, who had the ways and means to realize a building twenty-one stories high that would become one of the most famous landmarks in the city. The Fuller Company was backed in this endeavor by Winfield A. Stratton, who had also made his fortune in Colorado gold mining. To flaunt his great wealth, he wanted to build a palatial residence for himself in Cripple Creek. He traveled to Chicago to commission the architectural firm of Daniel H. Burnham and Company and the builder and general contractor George A. Fuller. They were able to interest Stratton instead in leaving his mark by building the country's tallest office building in New York City.

Although Stratton invested his money in this venture, George A. Fuller became the owner of the Flatiron Building, where he maintained his offices for twenty years. The building bore his name during this time, even though early records show that Burnham and Fuller had referred to the structure as the Flatiron on the building's original plans. When the building was sold in 1925 and a new Fuller Building was erected at the corner of 57th Street and Madison Avenue, the Flatiron Building took on its official name. In the 57th Street lobby, Fuller imbedded a detailed mosaic of his beloved triangular Flatiron. The name often appeared in print as two words (Flat Iron) or hyphenated (Flat-iron), and was adopted because the shape of the plot of land upon which it was to be built resembled the utilitarian flat iron.

The Flatiron Building was not Daniel Burnham's introduction to Madison Square. He had been

149 *The former St. Germaine, now the Cumberland Apartments. On its north facade, considered at the time to be the most valuable advertising space in the city, the* New York Times *chose to install a sign bearing their slogan, which has survived to this very day — "All the News That's Fit to Print." The lowest building, with the six arched windows along Broadway at 23rd Street, was the ticket office of the Erie Railroad.*

honored on March 25, 1893, directly across the park at Madison Square Garden's Concert Hall by Frederick Law Olmsted, for his extraordinary contribution as director of works for the World's Columbian Exposition in Chicago. He had been appointed chief of construction of the project and had led a group of noted architects in creating the main buildings for the exposition. It was said of Burnham that he "inspired confidence in all who came within the range of his positive and powerful personality," and considering his experience with building Chicago skyscrapers in the French Renaissance style, he had the perfect credentials to attempt this daring building at that time.

In designing the Flatiron, the architect's challenges were many. He not only had to address the advantages of the conspicuous site — in the middle of the crossing of Fifth Avenue and Broadway — by maximizing its magnitude, altitude and detachment, but also had to minimize its major disadvantage — the sharp edge of the apex at 23rd Street. The massive structure that was to emerge from this plot would be viewed, according to an article in *Architectural Record*, in much the same way as a piece of sculpture, "all around . . . all at once . . . and at a distance."

150 *The Flatiron under construction, with the outer walls of what appear to be the sixth and seventh floors literally being applied to the structural steelwork, while the unclad framework of the floors above and below remain exposed.*

151 *Nearing completion, a daring shot from the top of the Flatiron looking down on Fifth at 23rd and Broadway. The bold shadow points to the Fifth Avenue Hotel.*

Keeping all this in mind, it was necessary for the architect to produce a building that multiplied the value of the bit of ground at its base, described as a "stingy piece of pie" many times over. It appears that the actual design of the Flatiron, although a product of Burnham's large architectural firm, was not actually executed by Burnham himself. The article "Late Works by Burnham and Sullivan," written for the Art Institute of Chicago's *Museum Studies* in 1984, indicates that drawings in the institute's collection credit the design and detailing of the building to Frederick P. Dinkelberg. Burnham conceived the idea of constructing a steel skeleton of columnar design to rest at frequent intervals on spread footings. He utilized connecting beams and girders as supports for the panel fillers of brick or fireproofing for the walls and partitions. The heavy knee bracing was used on every floor, making this building one of the most overbuilt structures in the city. The twenty stories rose 307 feet high and its foundation was 35 feet deep. It utilized 3,680 tons of structural steelwork, designed by the consulting engineers Purdy and Henderson and manufactured by the American Bridge Company.

Spectators watched as outer walls of rusticated limestone and terra-cotta were being hung on the massive steel skeleton from the top down. This kind of construction allowed for the walls at the base to be no thicker than the walls at the top of the building. The manufacturer of the building's facade material was able to match the tint of the terra-cotta to the warm gray of the limestone base. The detail towards the top was noted to be well adjusted in scale and well adapted to its altitude. The frieze of the fourth story was effective at emphasizing a transitional member of the building's composition. Upon its completion, the Flatiron Building was clearly visible from the entrance of Central Park at 59th Street.

The Flatiron Building was landmarked on September 20, 1966. In 1979 the National Register of Historic Places described its physical attributes as follows:

The exterior of the Flatiron Building is divided into three sections: base, shaft and capital. The lower five floors comprise the base and are in turn divided into three sections by heavy stone entablatures. The centers of both the Fifth Avenue and Broadway facades are each high-lighted by a double story, arched entrance surround[ed] by engaged columns. Colossal pilasters which separate the display windows on the first two floors are composed of alternating blocks of smooth-faced and patterned stone. The third and fourth stories are simpler with piers and spandrels of rusticated limestone while the fifth story is heavily ornamented with abstract floral motifs and medallions containing faces or fleur-de-lys. The twelve story shaft is covered on much of its surface by richly decorated terra cotta . . . The capital of the building, from the 18th floor to the 21st, is again divided into three sections by protruding stone entablatures. . . . The projecting heavy entablature of the roof . . . is decorated with a dentil pattern. Capping the entire building is a stone balustrade, with squat piers interspersed throughout.

The encircling balustrade meets at the northernmost end with a three-dimensional relief of two figures flanking a shield bearing the monogram of George A. Fuller.

152 *In 1990 the Flatiron sculpture, in total disrepair, was removed as part of the building's restoration. It was not until 2001 that the newly fabricated "Prow Medallion," the name given to the sculpture's re-creation project, was replaced by Newmark under the guidance of building manager, Edward O'Grady.*

Allen Barr of Town House Restoration, Maspeth, New York, supervised the fabrication of the new sculpture from GFRC, Glass Fiber Reinforce Concrete. Created by French sculptor Betty Martin, a full-size pattern was made utilizing photographic materials, many supplied by Madison Square resident photographer Jerzy Koss. The completed piece was installed by Yates Restoration Group Ltd. under the direction of Richard H. Balser, Engineers.

NYC
LANDMARK

THE FLATIRON BUILDING

175 FIFTH AVENUE

SEPTEMBER 20 1966

NEW YORK STATE AND NATIONAL REGISTERS OF HISTORIC PLACES

1980

153 *The completed Flatiron Building sported window awnings to help keep the fully exposed offices cooler on hot summer days.*

THE COWCATCHER

The one-story glass protrusion on the ground level at 23rd Street appears to have been somewhat of an afterthought. Some of the first renderings of the building show a round gazebo-like structure, totally freestanding, placed in front of the rounded building facade. The building's original design was for three entrances, each flanked by decorative columns. There would be one entrance on Fifth, one entrance on Broadway and a third entrance at 23rd Street. The Fifth Avenue entrance brought the two columns close together, allowing for what appeared to be the width of a single entry, such as that of a revolving door. After the structure was completed, this entrance was sealed off as a public entryway and the attached odd addition was built. It became known as the "cowcatcher" since it was reminiscent of the inclined frame attached to the front of a locomotive for removing cattle in the path of a train. High winds that caused so much distress at this location

might have proven this entryway impractical. This unique building addition was a bonus to any business that rented the northern end of the ground floor because its almost unusable space made it a perfect display window. The first of these tenants that was into high visibility, the United Cigar Company, proclaimed themselves to be the building's most "famous tenant." Sharing their space was the popular tour company Seeing New York.

Some cowcatcher tenants for whom display was not an issue simply painted the glass from inside. For many years the bright red glass with the bold name of the Astra Trading Company was enough to call attention to this company's location.

When the cowcatcher was restored in 1990, the windows were replaced, its flat roof was refinished with a new scalloped edging and its ironwork was painted black. For the first time in many years, the original 23rd Street columned entrance was revealed, encased in the building's rounded glass point. Its first tenant, the C. P. Company, an upscale men's clothing store, did little to enhance this space with its displays. The company even managed to mask the newly exposed architectural detailing. However, its tenant as of this writing, Sprint Communications, has a rather large flattened stylized globe that, when illuminated at night, showcases not only its business but also this unusual space. Perhaps Sprint's message is that this spot is not only the "the center of the United States" but conceivably "the center of the world."

Offices in the narrow rounded portion of the building proper had a somewhat awkward space to fill. In 1902 *Architectural Digest* described the effects of this space on a potential occupant: "He can, perhaps, find wall space within for one roll-top desk without overlapping the windows . . . But suppose he needed a bookcase? Undoubtedly he has a highly eligible place from which to view processions. But for the transaction of business? And the aesthetic effect is even more depressing. The wedge is blunted, by being rounded, to a width of five or six feet — possibly ten. . . . For the treatment of the tip is as additional and seems a wanton aggravation of the inherent awkwardness of the situation."

154 *The dramatic perspective of the cowcatcher from 23rd Street. The Flatiron holds its own, with the Twin Towers dwarfed in the background.*

155 *One of the first tenants of the northerly ground-floor space was the United Cigar Company.*

156 *In* The Real New York, *Rupert Hughes describes this sightseeing phenomenon at the time. "Round and round the town also go the 'Seeing New York' automobile coaches, packed with tourists, who are shown the sights under the guidance of a lecturer with a megaphone. Many New Yorkers, too, join these parties, and learn with amazement what store of interest has been gathering here unbeknownst while they were gadding Europe." Here a tour departs from the company's offices located on the ground floor of the Flatiron Building.*

ROOMS WITH LIGHT, AIR AND VIEWS

An observation deck and restaurant high above Madison Square afforded visitors to the Flatiron Building a panoramic view of the city, including glimpses of Central Park, the Statue of Liberty and the East River bridges. This penthouse space in the sky, with its broad vistas and uninterrupted light, was to be taken over by the Art Career School. The entire Flatiron Building, in fact, afforded most every office an abundance of natural daylight. One of its early tenants was *Munsey's* magazine. Frank Munsey's publishing firm occupied the eighteenth floor. In their July 1905 issue, after acclimating to their new space, they featured several illustrations of views from their offices — north, south, east and west — and a descriptive essay by Edgar Saltus. Following are three of his brief observations on the Flatiron:

157 *The Flatiron Restaurant located at the top of the building was a favorite tourist spot.*

Its front is lifted to the future. On the past its back is turned. Of what has gone before it is American in its unconcern. Monstrous yet infantile, it is a recent issue of the gigantic upheaval that is transforming the whole city, and which will end by making it a curiosity to which people will come and stare as they do at cataracts and big caves and great trees and fat women and whatever else is abnormal.

Evolution may be slow, but it is sure; yet however slow, it achieved an unrecognized advance when it devised buildings such as this. It is demonstrable that small rooms breed small thoughts. It will be demonstrable that as buildings ascend so do ideas. It is mental progress that skyscrapers engender. From these parturitions gods may really proceed — beings, that is, who, could we remain long enough to see them, would regard us as we regard the apes.

. . . For as you lean and gaze from the toppest floors on houses below, which from those floors seem like huts, it may occur to you that precisely as these huts were once regarded as supreme achievements, one of these days, from other higher floors, the Flatiron may seem a hut itself.

Although building heights continued to soar to record-breaking levels, none seemed to be able to diminish the stature of the Flatiron Building. More people came to look up at this curiosity than could ever get close enough to look down on it.

THE FLATIRON FOR SALE

In 1925 the Flatiron Building was sold by the Fuller Interests and Improvement Company to a syndicate representing banking and realty interests, headed by L. N. Rosenbaum and including W. S. Hammons Banker of Portland, Maine, David H. Knott of the Knott Hotels chain, and H. L. Clark of Utilities Power and Light Company. Together they formed the Flatiron Corporation. The assessed land value at this time was $1,025,000, with the building valued at $1,000,000.

In 1933 the *New York Times* reported that the Flatiron Building was purchased by the Equitable Life Assurance Society in a foreclosure action. Increased operating costs and interest, plus the effects of business decline in 1929, resulted in this purchase. They paid $100,000 to satisfy a lien of $1,238,727 in an action brought by Equitable against the Flatiron Corporation and others. Harry Helmsley, with the real-estate firm of Dwight-Helmsley, Inc., had occupied the entire nineteenth floor. In 1945 the real-estate firm of Helmsley Spear became the managing agent for the building and ran it until the building was taken over in 1996 by Newmark and Company Real Estate.

One of Newmark's copresidents, James Kuhn, first became enamored with the Flatiron when he had an office at the Met Life Building at One Madison Avenue. It was from there that he gazed longingly at the Flatiron and fell in love with it. Kuhn and his associates bought the building as "tenants in common," a form of ownership where every principal has the same voting rights, whether they own 99 percent or 1 percent. At that time, Leona Helmsley owned 18 percent and Helmsley-Spear was the leasing and managing agent. They were to run the Flatiron for the first two years that Newmark owned it. Today Newmark is the leasing and managing agent. At the close of the twentieth century, they replaced the six banks of original water-hydraulic elevators with electric ones, eliminating the bouncing ride that had jarred people for years.

As the years went on, a diverse mix of businesses made the Flatiron their home, from dentists to architects to designers to record companies to publishers to various arts organizations. This prestigious location remained a much sought-after business address, as witnessed by a popular mail-drop tenant who occupied an office on the eleventh floor for many years. However, according to a *New York Times* article published at the time of the building's restoration, it was predicted that by 1998 the Flatiron would house only two tenants, Springer-Verlag and St. Martin's Press, two major publishing companies that have made the building their home for more than twenty-five years. As of this writing, the two companies occupy over 95 percent of the building.

23 SKIDOO!

Soon after the building's erection in 1902, it is said that a very popular phrase was coined at this spot. It was here that gentlemen with a minute to spare would stop to gaze upon an upturned skirt. This pastime became so popular that a patrolman had to be assigned at the spot to keep the oglers moving along. Officers on the beat developed the expression "23 Skidoo" (meaning "scram" or "move on").

A lady's boot soon became synonomous with the phrase. If she did not appreciate the flirtatious overtures of one of the many Flatiron mashers, she was known to kindly give him " the boot."

158 *Many 23 Skidoo buttons were manufactured as this popular phrase caught on. This pinback bore the symbolic "boot."*

159 *An impatient wife awaits the arrival of her husband armed with a "flat iron." She believes he may be delayed by the feminine diversions around the other Flatiron.*

160 *An example of an amicable meeting. An early postcard such as this might contain a ditty such as, "To Madison Park / there let us go / and I to you / the way will show."*

THE WIND AND 23 SKIDOO

The intersection of Broadway and Fifth at 23rd Street was thought to be the windiest spot in town. Rumor spread upon the Flatiron's completion that it could be seen to sway in a high wind, and it was even reported in one paper that if the Flatiron were to topple over, it would reach Madison Avenue.

In 1904 Sir Philip Burne-Jones, in *Dollars and Democracy,* gave a rather graphic account of this newly created phenomenon:

One vast horror, facing Madison Square, is distinctly responsible for a new form of hurricane, which meets unsuspecting pedestrians as they reach the corner, causing them extreme discomfort. . . . When its effects first became noticeable, a little rude crowd of loafers and street arabs used to congregate upon the curb to jeer and gloat over the distress of ladies whose skirts were blown into their eyes as they rounded the treacherous corner. Hanging around this particular spot soon became a recognized and punishable offense.

The following account of a windy day was recorded on April 15, 1903, in the *New York World Telegram:*

Not since the Flatiron Building reared its lofty head at Twenty-Third and Broadway has the wind played such high jinks as yesterday. Officially it was an east wind but those who braved it at this particular spot in the city were willing to swear that it was east, west, north and south and all at the same moment. The police on duty at these points were kept busy all day long in rescuing women who had lost control of their movements and willy-nilly were being blown out of their course. Collisions between pedestrians were frequent, blow overs numerous, and hats and umbrellas soared skyward often. Mrs. Bertha Lyons was blown at Broadway and 22nd Street receiving contusions to the face and body. Dr. Thomas of N. Y. Hospital was called to attend her at the Bartholdi Hotel after which she took a cab to her home.

In another account of February 1903, a messenger was blown out into Fifth Avenue, where he was killed by a passing automobile. Local merchants had opposed the building and the great winds that this bulk of a building created. One such merchant, Gibson N. Vincent, sued for $5,000 worth of damages. November 28, 1950, brought with it "New York's Biggest Blow," which resulted in street-level windows in the cowcatcher caving in from gale-force winds. The winds today don't seem to be quite as severe, probably due to the higher structures that help distribute the strong air currents.

161 *The front cover of* Leslie's *magazine captures the violent winds around the Flatiron.*

162 *The more genteel version of the wind phenomenon that was known to reek havoc and cause heads to turn.*

RESTORATION

According to a *New York Times* article of July 21, 1991, the first cleaning of this landmark occurred in 1924. In 1950 the terra-cotta portion of the facade was steam-cleaned down through the fourth floor, and the remaining floors of limestone were given a coat of cleaner.

Although the exterior of the Flatiron was designated a landmark in 1966, the interior was never granted this status due to numerous renovations obliterating many of the original architectural appointments. The six original open-ironwork caged elevators were enclosed in the 1930s. The original vaulted ceiling in the lobby that created a tunnel-like effect from Fifth Avenue through to Broadway had been covered by a dropped ceiling, and the mahogany panels in which the revolving doors of its two entrances were set had been replaced by a combination of glass and stainless steel. In 1986, in an attempt to "modernize" the dropped ceiling, the original coffered vaulted ceiling was removed one evening and work commenced on a new dropped acoustic-tile ceiling. Fortunately, enough people had a chance to glance at the dramatic vaulting to know that there had to be a better solution, but unfortunately they did not have time to save it. Objections were raised and work was quickly halted. The lobby remained in its transitional state for several months before revised plans began for a new plaster vaulted ceiling — more in keeping with the original design but still, many voiced, not an appropriate solution for so prestigious a building.

The Flatiron's first major restoration began in July 1990 and proceeded in three phases. The first phase was the restoration of the cowcatcher. This was followed by phase two in the early summer of 1991, which included the steam-cleaning of the entire building. The task took place over a period of several months, providing passersby with breathtaking evening views of workers clad in yellow slickers illuminated on swinging scaffolds, sometimes all but obscured by the steam bouncing off the facade. By day their efforts revealed a graphic black-and-white striated facade — cleaned strips juxtaposed with strips holding years of accumulated soot. The million-dollar project was overseen by Hurley and Farinella, architects, and Richard Balger, engineer. Once the building was cleaned, the third and final phase commenced: pointing (scratching out old mortar) and completely restoring the masonry. The overall effect was a startlingly clean Flatiron, though some preservationists think the process to achieve this end might have been too harsh, exposing the facade to possible further damage.

The truly final phase of this restoration will be the replacement of the building's "Prow Medallion" high above 23rd Street, to be installed by Newmark and Company Real Estate in 2001 in time to celebrate the Flatiron's one hundreth anniversary in 2002.

163 *Broad stripes appeared upon the building's facade during its extensive cleaning project.*

STIEGLITZ, STEICHEN AND THE FLATIRON

Edward Steichen had maintained his photography studio at 291 Fifth Avenue at 30th Street, and when he decided to vacate in 1905, he encouraged Alfred Stieglitz to take over the space to house the Photo-Secession, a photographic society that Stieglitz had founded in 1902. Eventually the "Little Galleries of the Photo-Secession" became known simply as "291" and from its three tiny rooms exhibited not only photographs but also avant-garde painting and sculpture. The gallery and the society existed until 1917 when the building was torn down. Within easy view of the newly built Flatiron, both Stieglitz and Steichen were drawn to the unusual structure, and each created his own memorable image of the building, Stieglitz in 1903 and Steichen in 1904.

The following exchange between Alfred Stieglitz and his father is quoted by Dorothy Norman in *Alfred Stieglitz: An American Seer:*

I remember my father coming upon me as I was photographing in the middle of Fifth Avenue. "Alfred", he said, "how can you be interested in that hideous build-ing?" "Why, Pa," I replied, "it is not hideous, but the new America. The Flatiron is to the United States what the Parthenon was to Greece."

LITTLE-KNOWN FACTS ABOUT THE FLATIRON BUILDING

• Although the Flatiron Building gives the illusion of being an isosceles triangle, it is, in fact, a right triangle. This can best be seen as you approach the building from the north and view its Broadway frontage from the east side of Fifth Avenue.

• In 1974 the *Guinness Book of Records* sponsored a diving event at the Flatiron Building. Henry La Mothe leaped into a small pool placed atop the cowcatcher. He plunged into the water from a forty-foot ladder and, upon his descent to the sidewalk, was greeted by his wife, who presented him with a cake to mark his seventieth birthday.

• In 1979, when Katherine Hepburn was interviewed on the television program *60 Minutes,* she was asked what it was like to be a legend. She replied that it was like being some grand old building you pass and look up at. The interview was about to

164 *In this photo of the Flatiron Building, Alfred Stieglitz captures the famous landmark from Madison Square Park with a tree in the foreground that suggests the right triangle of the build-ing in plan.*

165 *A backlit Flatiron Building as pho-tographed by Edward Steichen and seen from the west side of Madison Square Park, with a cabby awaiting a fare.*

166 *The floorplan for the first floor of the Flatiron Building.*

OPPOSITE

167 *Many visitors to New York were so taken by this new peculiar building that they often wrote messages about their impressions — some more poetic and expressive than others.*

*There was a young boy from Rye
Who saw this building so high,
He walked to the top
and then couldn't stop
Now they're looking for him in the sky*

continue with another question, when Morley Safer backed up and asked her if she had to compare herself to a building, which one would it be? Hepburn responded without much hesitation, "The Flatiron Building."

• The Flatiron was the most popular image to ever be produced on a picture postcard. This phenomenon was the result of the building's construction coinciding with the introduction of the postcard. There are probably more than five hundred different images of this famous structure that found their way onto these postcards, and oftentimes a little artistic license was taken by postcard manufacturers. Through retouching they could make the building taller then it really was, create their favorite time of day for the building's environment (turning day into night and vice versa), and on many occasions even add and delete people from a scene. The Flatiron Building was the favorite card of those who came to visit the city for the first time. It was an impressive image to mail home to family and friends. They not only commented about the extraordinary shape and height of the building, but also often wrote in their brief messages about the high and gusty winds.

168 *As if receiving an award, this lady is bearing a replica of the Flatiron representing the state of New York.*

THE GREAT ONCOMING FLATIRON

The Flatiron Building has often been likened to a massive ship moving northward from its 23rd Street berth. This illusionary attribute, has helped to keep the Flatiron one of the most notable and recognizable icons depicted on the New York City skyline. Its verticality long surpassed, few skyscrapers could rival its horizontality and suggestion of progressive movement. The following observations best capture the impression:

"...There is the great oncoming Flat-Iron building, and behind it the racing clouds like waves of the sea propelling it towards me! Yes, this beautiful new Flat-Iron seems to be moving majestically up the Avenue to meet me, and my own weariness lifts with its reflected light, with wonder, and with a feeling of actual movement — a quick, thrilling imagining of voyage to come!"

— Susan N. Polsifer, *A House in Time,* 1958

"Never in the history of mankind has a little triangular piece of real estate been utilized in such a raffiné manner. . . . It is a building without a main facade. . . . And we would not be astonished . . . if the whole triangular block would suddenly begin to move northward through the crowd of pedestrians and traffic of our two leading thoroughfares, which would break like the waves of the ocean on the huge prow-like angle."

— Sadakichi Hartmann, "An Esthetical Dissertation," *Camera Work,* October 1903

"With the trees of Madison Square covered with fresh snow, the Flatiron impressed me as never before. It appeared to be moving toward me like the bow of a monster ocean steamer — a picture of new America still in the making."

— Alfred Stieglitz, as quoted by Dorothy Norman in *Alfred Stieglitz: An American Seer,* 1973

"On August 24, a section of Broadway collapsed and filled with water. In a rare instance of architectural justice, wavelets lapped at the Flatiron Building's snubnosed prow."

— Guy Trebay, "The Hole Story," *Village Voice,* July 6, 1983

7

PARADES, PROCESSIONS
& GATHERINGS

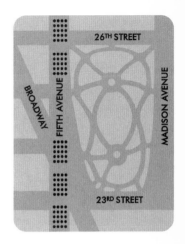

The story of Madison Square began with a description of the immense open space between 23rd and 34th Streets and 3rd and 7th Avenues known as "The Parade," and its use as a military parade ground during the War of 1812. The Middle Road, later renamed Fifth Avenue, not only divided this huge plot in half but also the island of Manhattan from Washington Square up to the Harlem River. As the area was reduced in size, Fifth Avenue was to maintain its strong relationship to Madison Square Park by creating its westerly border. Merging with Broadway at 25th Street, this juncture was chosen for the burial site of General William J. Worth in 1857. Fifth Avenue's central location soon became the perfect venue for public gatherings and, before long, the city's primary parade route. At first Fifth Avenue maintained its original decorum by hosting more solemn military and funeral processions. In time it attracted more colorful events, becoming a place for a multiplicity of public, political and festive celebrations. Bleachers flanked both sides of Fifth Avenue along the wide expanse of Madison Square, with a main reviewing stand placed near the Worth Monument (fig. 72). Most parades of note came to a halt at the general's monument to be reviewed and formally welcomed by visiting dignitaries and honored guests. Major celebrations were often accompanied by elaborate decoration, and, on several occasions, the erection of triumphal arches. These temporary arches set a dramatic stage for great pomp and circumstance.

In *New York — Not So Little and Not So Old,* Sarah Lockwood observes, "Fifth Avenue is preeminently the street of parades. This is a free country. If we feel like parading — and we do — nothing shall stop us, and Fifth Avenue is the street we like to do it on." And so, most every conceivable newsworthy event became cause for a parade, and Madison Square, from the 1850s to the early 1900s, became one of the most favored spots from which to view or join in the festivities. Most parades were structured to be seen from the sidelines. There were, however, more-casual gatherings that attracted crowds who came to participate. These included the circus parades of P. T. Barnum, who marched his menagerie of animals through the city streets to Madison Square Garden, their temporary home on the park; the fashion parades favored by the promenaders of Madison Square, who in the early 1800s broke from their daily walks in the park and joined fellow fashion-conscious New Yorkers to stroll up Fifth Avenue to 59th Street in the first Easter Parades; and throngs of celebrants laden with toys and gifts who came out to greet old Saint Nicholas, who had taken his place upon the grand reviewing stand in front of the general's monument.

Regardless of where a parade commenced, be it north or south of Madison Square, the crossing of the two great thoroughfares of Fifth Avenue and Broadway (which itself became a popular course) allowed for a variation of parade routes. It was here that these long processions could switch with ease from Broadway to Fifth and vice versa. Whether it was the beginning, the middle or the culmination of an event, it was here that these sometimes endless lines of marchers and floats came to pause and be greeted and cheered by crowds of supporters and well-wishers.

The crowds were always heavy along the parade route, and finding a viewing place was a challenge. Those in the rear would bring a wooden box to stand on. Others purposely walked right on the parade route so that when they were asked to take a place on the sidewalk they could push in front of people who had held their front-row position for hours. Police were aware of this trick and often ushered these interlopers onto side streets. A lucky few were able to find a place in the reviewing stands, and many paid large sums of money to secure an uninterrupted view of the passing pageantry from the upper floors and rooftops of homes and other buildings lining the parade route.

In her 1978 book *Fifth Avenue: A Very Social History,* Kate Simon gives the following account:

Seats in stands along Fifth Avenue went to the chosen, rich and political. One room in a Fifth Avenue house near Twenty-sixth Street cost five hundred dollars for the afternoon; one window jammed with dozens of faces took in three hundred dollars and a four-story building with a spread of windows on the Avenue collected three thousand.

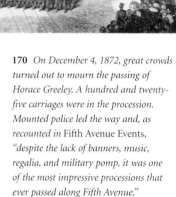

THE SOMBER PROCESSIONS

Columns of soldiers and bands marched to honor returning troops, celebrate war heroes or commemorate important anniversaries. They also accompanied the funeral processions of Lincoln, Greeley, Grant, McKinley, Farragut, Arthur and Sherman when their remains were carried through the streets and thousands turned out to pay their final respects. These occasions often brought city land and sea traffic to a halt while church bells near and far filled the air.

THE TORCHLIGHT PARADES

There were numerous evening parades and processions illuminated by handheld torches, lanterns and Roman candles and augmented by ambitious fireworks displays. These often called attention to political issues or were staged in support of a prospective political candidate. One such evening parade in 1860 celebrated the presidential campaign of Lincoln. He was once again feted upon his second inauguration on March 6, 1865, in a spectacular procession from City Hall Park to Madison Square. Other such events celebrated the visits of foreign dignitaries. One of the earliest parades, honoring the visit of the Prince of Wales on October 13, 1860, seemed to have been known by at least two names: the Firemen's Parade and the Torchlight Procession. On that evening at half past

170 *On December 4, 1872, great crowds turned out to mourn the passing of Horace Greeley. A hundred and twenty-five carriages were in the procession. Mounted police led the way and, as recounted in* Fifth Avenue Events, *"despite the lack of banners, music, regalia, and military pomp, it was one of the most impressive processions that ever passed along Fifth Avenue."*

171 *The funeral procession of General Sherman on February 19, 1891, as it passed the Fifth Avenue Hotel. It was said that more than eleven thousand marched on this solemn occasion. Two years prior, Sherman had taken the same route but in the opposite direction as a participant in the George Washington Centenary parade.*

OPPOSITE

172 *Crowds gather in front of the Fifth Avenue Hotel to celebrate the July 4th centennial in 1876.*

THE INDEPENDENCE DAY CENTENNIAL CELEBRATION

JULY 4TH, 1876

Crowds celebrated with yet another festive illuminated spectacle commemorating the centennial of the signing of the Declaration of Independence. Homes were decorated by very simple means. The lower three panes of twelve-pane window glass prevalent at the time were covered with red, white and blue tissue, behind which was placed a lit candle. Fireworks displays were in abundance, including a festive celebration in front of the Fifth Avenue Hotel and the Worth Monument, reviewed by Mayor Wickham and featuring illuminated images of the Statue of Liberty and the Liberty Bell.

Following are several exerpts from The *New York Tribune,* Thursday July 4, 1876, that bring to life this memorable day on Madison Square:

BY DAY:

"The New-York Club made a good display of national colors, a great ensign flying from the roof and a large flag hanging out of every window on three sides of the building. It also had the novel feature of a painting, by Lavastere, decorative painter of the Paris Grand Opera, of the proposed French monument of Liberty to be placed in New York Harbor, in dimensions 22 by 36 feet. This was placed over the entrance between the bacony and the cornice, and fronting the Worth Monument, and it was illuminated by a strong reflected light during the passage of the torchlight procession."

"The Fifth Avenue Hotel was decorated in plain but costly style, and on a broad plan, corresponding well with its massive appearance.

The material throughout was genuine bunting. A 46-foot flag flew from the main staff, and a 30-foot flag hung from a staff over the cornice above the principal entrance, to which, from the cornice, were drawn two triple-colored streamers of bunting each 90 feet long. The same material was used to drape the balustrade of the portal balcony, which was also decorated with five flags 16 feet long. Eighty-four flags of equal size were hung, one above the other, out of the corner windows fronting on Fifth-ave. and on Broadway. Two large flags were flying before each entrance on Twenty-third-st. and Twenty-fourth-st."

"The Brunswick Hotel displayed a large flag from the staff, and the ensigns of foreign nations along the cornice."

"The Union League Club House displayed an immense American flag. Strings of flags of all nations were attached to the top of the staff and to the cornice. The balconies on the Madison-square side were tastefully decorated with festooned flags and bunting and stands of flags grouped to form a shield. . . .'"

"Gilmore's Garden bore flags on the turret and from the cornices. . . .'"

"Kurtz, the photographer, decorated his building with a handsome transparency painted by himself, and with two large American and, German flags flying from the roof.

"The residence of Col. Hawkins, Chairman of the Centennial Committee, at No. 16 West Twenty-third-st. [neighboring house to the Wharton residence], was decorated with a large flag hanging over the entrance, and smaller flags hung from the upper story windows."

BY NIGHT:

"A strong calcium light was placed near the foot of the Worth monument in such a position as to bring out the pictures to good advantage. Two medalions bearing the figures '1776' and '1876', and a large star of red, white, and blue gas-jets were seen on the Broadway side of this club-house."

". . .The Fifth Avenue Hotel fronting on Broadway and Twenty-third and Twenty-fourth-sts., was lighted with red, white and blue lamps, five lamps being placed in each window, producing a beautiful effect as from the park opposite."

"The windows of the Albemarle Hotel and the front of the building occupied by C. G. Gunther's Sons [a fur dealer and furrier], on Fifth Ave., near Twenty-third-st., were similarly lighted, the former displaying about 400 lamps, and the latter 250."

"The Union League Club House displayed about 400 lamps, similar to those in the different hotels."

"At the Kurtz Art Gallery, on Twenty-third-st., facing the park, there was a large transparency of Columbia holding the flag of the country, with one foot on a line, symbolical of power. On one side of the transparency was a portrait of Washington, and on the other a portrait of Lincoln. The front of the building was covered with 800 lamps."

"The Erie ticket office, at the corner of Broadway and Twenty-third-st., also displayed about 400 lamps of different colors and 6 locomotive headlights."

six, participants began to gather and companies fell into order by eight. The avenues, streets and squares were dense with onlookers. The prince was to view this spectacle from the balcony of the Fifth Avenue Hotel. When the advance guard of the firemen approached Madison Square, the prince and Police Commissioner Kennedy stepped onto the balcony and were cheered by enthusiastic crowds. Hook and Ladder Company No. 12 directed brilliant beams of calcium light upon the prince, creating a spotlight effect and bathing him in a dazzling glare of white light. Bands played the British anthem and thousands danced in the streets with flaring torches. One hundred and four engine companies, which included five thousand uniformed firemen and their apparatus and band, paraded past the balcony of the Fifth Avenue Hotel. As each company passed, they sent a torrent of shells skyward from their engine's smokestack, lighting up the dark October night.

THE BOYS IN BLUE

In late October of 1880, the Republican Party staged one of the more spectacular evening affairs in support of General James A. Garfield. This torchlight parade, which featured the Boys in Blue, was reviewed by General Ulysses S. Grant. The comparison of the Boys in Blue to Garfield, all representing honest and sturdy character, was the objective of this event. It was said their careful

173 *The Boys in Blue greeted by General Ulysses Grant from the viewing stand at the Worth Monument. The arm of Lady Liberty holding her torch aloft amid the supportive crowds in Madison Square Park was a moving and dramatic sight.*

training enabled them to turn successfully to any new form of duty. These young men went from the office and workshop, from college and common school to defend their country and returned to the pursuit of peace, as Garfield had done. As reported in *Harper's Weekly*, October 30, 1880, "Such men are the hope and stay of the country. It is the citizen volunteer who is the bulwark of the nation."

THE BUSINESSMEN'S PARADE

The Businessmen's, or Sound Money, Parades were staged in support of political candidates and their issues and usually took place prior to elections. Many were held after dark, with business wagons featuring the names of candidates, slogans and campaign promises emblazoned on transparent textile sheets and lit from within the wagons. They were equipped with bells that tolled as they lumbered along the cobblestone streets. Often large banners were stretched across the broad streets bearing portraits of candidates and party emblems. The first Businessmen's parade in 1884 was arranged by the Democrats and Independents for Grover Cleveland, with over 35,000 men marching down Fifth Avenue. Cleveland stood bare headed in the not-too-friendly weather, looking impassive and stolid among the enthusiastic shouting paraders. The November 2, 1884, *New York Times* reported that "from four o'clock until seven Mr. Cleveland maintained his position." When the publishers' section, led by Joseph Keppler of *Puck*, reached the reviewing stand near 25th Street, Roscoe Conkling, who had served in the United States Senate as a Republican representative for New York State, stepped out onto the balcony of number One West 25th Street (the Hoffman House, where he maintained a residence), placed his hand in the breast of his coat and unofficially reviewed the parade.

The largest and longest of these parades took place on October 31, 1896, the Saturday before Election Day. Over 100,000 marchers in support of William McKinley and a protective tariff and gold standard made their way from lower Broadway, past the reviewing stand at Madison Square, and up to 40th Street. From 11 A.M. to 6:30 P.M., an estimated crowd of one million gathered along the parade route to view the proceedings.

THE DEDICATION OF THE STATUE OF LIBERTY

On October 28, 1886, the dedication of the Statue of Liberty took place, with a parade on the river and a parade on land. Madison Square played host to visiting dignitaries, with the American delegation at the Hoffman House and the French delegation at the adjacent Fifth Avenue Hotel. The day of the parade, 21,000 marchers passed the reviewing stands at the Worth Monument as they headed south to the Battery. T*he Arm of the Statue of Liberty,* which had stood most surrealistically in the park for almost eight years, had been removed from Madison Square in 1885 in order to complete the statue.

174 *Decoration Day, which we know today as Memorial Day, was established in 1868 to honor the Civil War dead. In 1884 President Chester Arthur reviewed the parade at Madison Square, followed by President Grover Cleveland in 1885. Cleveland's appearance was captured in the June 13, 1885, issue of* Harper's Weekly.

ELECTION NIGHT

On each election night, thousands of onlookers poured into Madison Square to watch election results as they were tabulated and announced by means of a "magic lantern" that projected slides onto the side of the St. Germaine Hotel, the Flatiron's predecessor.

One of the sponsors of an election night was the *New York Times*. It was the idea of Adolph S. Ochs to set up the apparatus in the park to bring the voters' results directly to the people. He thought the high visibility at this juncture was so good that he later decided to feature a slide projection with the words "All the News That's Fit to Print" (fig. 149). That slogan is still featured on the front page of the *Times* today.

The Fifth Avenue Hotel, at 23rd and Fifth Avenue, was home to the Republican Party, and the neighboring Hoffman House, at 24th and Broadway, served as center for the Democratic Party. At the close of every presidential election in the 1890s, the returns of each party were received at their respective hotels. Charley Mahoney, betting commissioner at the time, frequently held huge

175 *Election night results were projected from Madison Square Park onto a banner set up on the ticket offices of the Erie Railroad, which occupied the most northerly portion of the triangular site at 23rd Street, Fifth and Broadway. The illumination in this November 17, 1888, Harper's Weekly engraving proclaims, "Harrison carries the state by 12,000."*

OPPOSITE

176 *The tradition of projecting Election Day results continued well after the appearance of the Flatiron Building with a screen set up on the building's cowcatcher as seen here on the cover of the November 8, 1906, issue of Leslie's Weekly.*

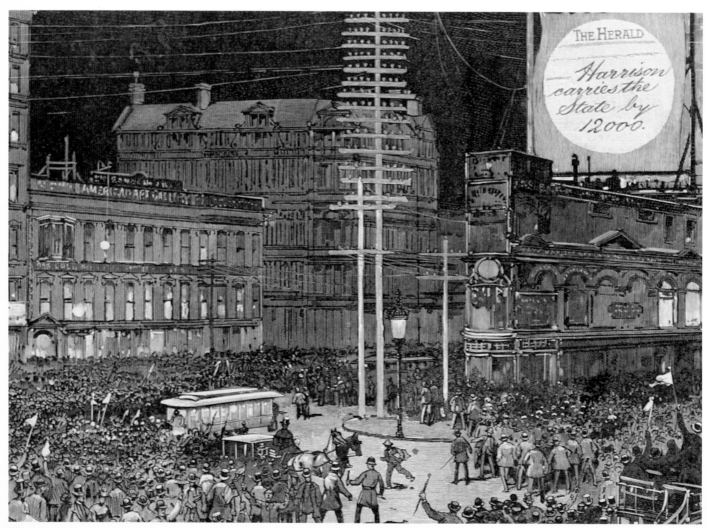

cash wagers on sporting events and election results. On election night, one had only to venture to the front door of the hotel and look over to the park to learn the outcome of one's wager.

This tradition continued into the early 1900s, and election results continued to be shown in Madison Square and on a screen erected on the Flatiron's cowcatcher. One of the first elections after the appearance of the Flatiron in 1902 brought with it a most unfortunate accident. William Randolph Hearst had come from San Francisco and set up an office at 1123 Broadway, at the corner of 25th Street. Not content in running the country from the pages of his newspapers, he decided to run for office. On election night, people gathered to watch the returns and a spectacular fireworks display. A little before 10 P.M., a nine-inch firework ignited prematurely inside a cast-iron mortar. When the mortar burst, it accidentally set off several bombs. Crowds became trapped in Madison Square Park and, as a result, twelve people lost their lives and hundreds more were injured. Although he won the election, the catastrophe haunted Hearst for the rest of his life.

THE CENTENNIAL CELEBRATION OF
GEORGE WASHINGTON'S INAUGURATION

The mid-1880s brought much excitement and preparation for the commemoration of the hundredth anniversary of George Washington's first inaugural as president on April 30, 1789. New York City had served as his early headquarters in the War of Independence and scene of his return from the end of the war, and it was to this city that he came to take his oath of office. The New-York Historical Society proposed ceremonies marking the centennial. In 1887 New Yorkers organized themselves into several committees. William Rhinelander Stewart, a resident at the northwest corner of Washington Square, conceived of a temporary arch to be erected over lower Fifth Avenue. Other temporary arches were planned for Wall Street and Madison Square at Fifth Avenue and 23rd and 26th Streets. Stanford White was commissioned by the Centennial Art and Exhibition Committee to design the Washington Square Arch at the foot of Fifth Avenue. It, too, was intended to be temporary, but it became so beloved that funds were eventually raised to construct the arch as a permanent monument.

The 1889 centennial celebration centered around three days of festivities. President Benjamin Harrison was rowed by thirteen sailors in a decorated barge from Elizabeth, New Jersey, to the foot of Wall Street to open the celebration. Events included naval and military parades, civic receptions, church services, an industrial and civic parade, an open-air concert, an exhibition of Washington memorabilia, a centennial ball and much more.

177 *One of a pair of temporary arches erected at Madison Square at 23rd Street and Fifth Avenue. The second arch can be partially seen to the extreme left, just above the Fifth Avenue Hotel clock.*

THE FOUR HUNDREDTH ANNIVERSARY OF COLUMBUS'S DISCOVERY OF AMERICA

The year 1892 marked the four hundredth anniversary of the discovery of America. At that time in New York, Columbus symbolized freedom to millions of Italians, Germans, Russians, Jews, Hungarians and Irish. On October 10, the day of the celebration, Mayor Hugh Grant was to lead thousands of schoolchildren down Fifth Avenue. Stanford White made his mark as a "civic decorator" with his efforts for the anniversary. Perry Belmont, chairman of the Sub-Committee on Art, appointed an Honorary Advisory Committee that included Stanford White, Richard Morris Hunt, Augustus Saint-Gaudens, John La Farge, William Merritt Chase, Louis C. Tiffany and John Quincy Adams Ward. White was appointed to create the decorations for Fifth Avenue, the main parade route. White, Hunt and La Farge were charged with selecting designs for temporary arches, and White and Tiffany published a pamphlet advising property owners along the avenue on how to appropriately decorate their stores, clubs and houses:

The question of color is most important, and we therefore urge a simple and concentrated color scheme. The keynote in each case should be confined to one color, if possible, and not a mixture of red, white, blue, yellow and green. This is always objectionable. Let the basis of the decoration never be more than two colors, confining the American color to a single spot. Of all colors yellow and white are the most effective as groundwork and a foil for spots. The Spanish colors, red and yellow, are, of course, appropriate in this instance and should be used occasionally.

During this period White worked practically nonstop and spent whatever free time he had taking refuge in his Madison Square Garden tower studio. During this intense period of work he claimed it was "the Roof Garden and the Ballet Girls" that cheered him up. The New York Art Committee supervised the erection of a statue of Columbus at 59th Street, Broadway, and Eighth Avenue.

The committee had also authorized two temporary arches on Fifth Avenue. The arch at 59th Street, a high wooden structure over which was fashioned papier-mâché figures, at the southeastern corner of Central Park, was designed by a young Columbia College architectural student, Harry Hertz. For 22nd Street, White created an elaborate trellis arch supported by twelve columns twenty feet high, decorated with flags, banners, and bunting and filled at night with lighted lanterns. In between were White's decorations — one block entirely yellow, the next white, and the third red and yellow.

From 22nd Street northward to 34th Street along Fifth Avenue, White had 100 sixty-foot poles erected. They were topped by spheres and eagles, adorned with flags, streamers, and shields bearing the arms of Isabella, Ferdinand and Columbus, and supported Venetian lanterns on wires strung across the street. It was reported that "the delicately tinted lights stretched away until they were dim in the distance and twinkled like as many stars." Unfortunately, most of this effect had waned before the pageant reached this destination. White arranged, at his own expense, to have the Madison Square Garden Tower illuminated in red, white, blue and green, and to fill the evening sky with an elaborate fireworks display initiated from the roof garden. He hung Japanese lanterns from the trees in Madison Square Park, where, until past midnight of the third day, throngs waited for the historical pageant that (when it appeared) turned out to be an escort of police followed by a seemingly endless stream of bicycles. *Harper's Weekly* described the decorations as "a triumph — Mr. White should have a municipal Commissioner of Public Beauty created for him." The *Boston Globe* declared the affair a great success, "thanks to Stanford White, the master spirit, without whom very little that is decorative could be accomplished in New York."

It was estimated that two million, about one-thirtieth of the population of the United States, crowded into Fifth Avenue and Broadway and the side streets. Police Superintendent Byrnes had ordered the police on duty to refrain from using any force, except in self-defense. It was indeed a tribute to both his people and those gathered that no club was ever used. White also illuminated City Hall and had the Washington Memorial Arch lighted. Many took advantage of the superb view from atop this arch by breaking through the small door and winding their way up to the top. White paid dearly for his exuberance and dedication: a bleeding ulcer confined him to bed for several weeks following the celebration.

THE TRIUMPHAL DEWEY ARCH

The parade in August 1898 celebrating the end of the Spanish-American War could not quite match the colossal event a year later honoring Admiral George Dewey's return from his victory over the Spanish at the Battle of Manila Bay. Dewey was commemorated with a four-day celebration, from September 27–30. His achievements served as the first major step toward the arrival of the United States as a world force.

Three days of this event took place on the water and the fourth, the land parade, commenced at West 125th Street. The seven-mile drive proceeded down Riverside Drive to 72nd Street, then to Eighth Avenue and on to Central Park West. It continued down to Central Park Circle, known today as Columbus Circle, across 59th Street and down Fifth Avenue to Madison Square Park, where the admiral had taken his spot in the main reviewing stand at the Worth Monument. The parade, after passing through the new and temporary Dewey Arch, continued down Fifth Avenue and dispersed at Washington Square.

The *New York Daily Tribune* described the reviewing stand at the Worth Monument, commenting "the Admiral's booth . . . [was] surmounted by a canopy of blue and white. . . . At each corner was a wreath of laurels, and at intervals bronze eagles with outstretched pinions had been placed. Over twenty thousand pink roses were used in banking the rail." According to the *New York Herald*, the admiral gazed at the Dewey Arch from the base to the wings of *Victory,* a hundred feet above him. He started forward a little when he caught a glimpse of his own face on a medallion held by one of the figures. His air was that of a man who wondered if such a tribute were really meant for him. He looked across at the white pillars outlined against the green of the trees, which gave the impression that he was in some classic grove. It took over four hours for close to 31,000 men of the United States Navy, Army and the militia of various states to pass through the arch. Dewey attended to the endless acknowledgment of salutes from officers and rigidly obeyed the saluting of the passing flags. He was delivered a magnificent bouquet of orchids. Learning they had come from a lady viewing the proceedings from the Hoffman House windows, he gallantly turned and bowed in the direction of the unknown giver, and then without missing a beat was back saluting yet another flag.

The Dewey Arch was the most ambitious of all the temporary arches ever created. Charles R. Lamb (1863–1928), a specialist in ecclesiastical decorative art, designed it after the Arch of Titus in Rome.

178 *Admiral Dewey, the celebrated war hero who was welcomed back from his successful Battle of Manila Bay.*

OPPOSITE

179 *The elaborate Dewey Arch as it appeared September 30, 1899, looking up Fifth Avenue from West 24th Street to the left and Madison Square Park to the right. It was so well liked that an effort was made to raise funds to make it a permanent structure. Dewey viewed the parade from the viewing stand located just behind the arch in front of the Worth Monument. He rode in the parade as far as the stand, took his place there, and never passed through his own triumphal arch.*

TO THE GLORY OF THE AMERICAN NAVY
AND IN HONORING REAR ADMIRAL
A GRATEFUL PEOPLE LOOKING ON THEIR VALOR
HAS BUILT THIS ARCH IN DEWEY'S

The arch was created as part of an architectural and sculptural program with works by well-known sculptors such as Daniel Chester French, Karl Bitter and John Quincy Adams Ward. Ward's impressive quadriga atop the arch depicts seahorses drawing a ship, symbolizing *Victory on the Sea*. At the base of each face of the arch are four allegorical sculpture groups.

It was said that the Dewey Arch was incorrectly named. It was, in fact, a naval memorial arch commemorating not only Dewey but also John Manley, Stephen Decatur, John Paul Jones, Isaac Hull, Mathew C. Perry, Robert F. Stockton, David G. Farragut, and David D. Porter. These men represented all the wars in which the United States had been engaged from the Revolution to the time of this commemoration.

The most ironical part of the entire ceremony and parade was that on the day of the celebration, Admiral Dewey took his place in the viewing stand without passing through his own arch, making him the first victor in naval history not to pass through his own triumphal arch. An observer remarked, "What was the use of building a forty thousand dollar arch, if they did not take Dewey through it?" This unfortunate mishap was blamed on Charles Lamb's faulty design of the court colonnade, which looked complete in itself. The colonnade should have been the entrance leading to the approach of the arch but

instead was placed south of the arch, between 24th and 23rd Streets. The editor of *American Architect* said of the columns and the strips of cloth used to link them together that they looked "exactly as if the main arch were taking out some little pup columns for a walk, tied together with ribbons to prevent them from straying." The arch was a collaboration of the National Sculpture Society and the American Society of Mural Painters, and one year later these groups of artists were to work side by side once again on the Appellate Courthouse, where they were to create an impressive permanent collection of their artistic efforts.

The arch, which had been hastily constructed in six weeks and made from staff (plaster reinforced with hay or burlap fiber), was a great success; unfortunately, fundraising efforts, which included selling medallions stamped into the remains of the decaying plaster work, were not enough to re-create the permanent monument. Only $190,000 of the $500,000 needed was raised. In 1901, with the arch in total disrepair, Bradford Lee Gilbert, an architect for the South Carolina Interstate and West Indian Exposition, removed the arch and transported the large allegorical groups to Charleston, where they were placed around the Art Palace until the exposition closed in 1902 and the structure was demolished.

POLICE PARADE

The Police of New York City were given their very own parade, a custom that appears to have started sometime after the Civil War. It was held annually on the first day of June. About half the police force — 1,400 men — participated in the parade of 1885. Due to the investigation of police corruption in 1895, the parade was canceled, but it was reinstated the following year and continued into the twentieth century. Soon thereafter, this police event came to an end, but it remained customary for the police to head each city parade.

180 *The Police Parade passes the reviewing stand at the Worth Monument.*

THE VICTORY ARCH

With the United States' involvement in World War I, New York City was about to partake in numerous gatherings on Fifth Avenue — some sad and some joyous. At the outset, New Yorkers turned out on Fifth Avenue to cheer the departing troops. Patriotism was reflected in the city's restaurants and theaters as patrons rose to hear the playing of the national anthems of all the Allies. Fifth Avenue became the Avenue of Allies, its buildings streaming with flags.

In order to finance the war, the United States had to raise funds to not only pay for the cost of going to war but also for financial aid to our Allies. In addition to taxes and loans, five bond issues were floated to help raise money; the first four bonds were known as "Liberty Loans" and the last was known as the "Victory Loan." New Yorkers were able to buy bonds in Madison Square Park, where a small makeshift bank facade was temporarily erected. The Liberty Loan Parade and the Great Wake-up America Parade were held in 1917 to draw attention to the fundraising. Streets were filled with fluttering flags of Allies; streamers and banners draped the houses along the route. A *Valentine Manual* from 1920 described the event as "one of the greatest demonstrations ever witnessed in America" and referred to Fifth Avenue as "a monster canyon of wildly enthusiastic humanity." Several of these marches were enhanced by military sculptures set upon the cowcatcher of the Flatiron, which served as a rather unique pedestal.

The Victory Parade welcoming the troops home took place in 1919 and was both a grand and somber occasion. A commemorative brochure produced by the Mayor's Committee of Welcome to Home-coming Troops, outlined the festivities of the day. It included a letter from Field Marshal Douglas Haig, commander-in-chief of the British Armies, who briefly but glowingly addressed what the men had done at the critical juncture of the war. "On the 29th of September you took

181 *Crowds turn out for a farewell march to bid troops godspeed as they depart to fight in World War I.*

3 rd. Regiment
Farewell Parade
New York Aug. 30, 1917

part with great distinction in the great and critical attack which shattered the enemy's resistance in the Hindenberg Line and opened the road to final victory. . . . Since that date, through three weeks of almost continuous fighting, you advanced from one success to another, overcoming all resistance, beating off numerous counter-attacks, and capturing several thousand prisoners and many guns."

All New York turned out to welcome the troops returning from France. The regiments marched up to Madison Square and under the Victory Arch, which spanned Fifth Avenue at 25th Street. The arch stood in the middle of Fifth Avenue, with its west footing firmly planted on the site of the Worth Monument. The invited dignitaries took their places just opposite, at a park-side monument slightly south of the arch. The elaborate stand included a podium with graduated seating and ran along Fifth Avenue between 24th and 25th Streets. The procession of marchers continued past a commemorative court of pylons in front of the New York Public Library. The parade terminated under a "curtain of jewels" that were suspended from two white pillars that, when illuminated at night by colored searchlights, produced a spectacular effect. Unlike the Dewey Arch, there was little interest in preserving this arch as a permanent monument. It deteriorated quite rapidly and was removed soon after the event.

VICTORY PARADE at New York
The victorious 27th. Division carrying
The hugh service flag for its 1972 dead heros
And the gun caison bearing the large
floral wreath. March 25th., 1919.
©UNDERWOOD & UNDERWOOD

182 *The Victory Arch, a temporary structure erected to welcome the military back from World War I, as seen looking south. Besides the crowds that fill the streets, notice the hundreds of onlookers pressed into office windows along the route.*

OPPOSITE

183 *Throngs that lined the streets are seen in* Victory Day Parade, 1919 *through the eyes of Theresa Bernstein, an early modernist painter who managed to capture the vibrancy of the day. Joan Whalen, who represents Ms. Bernstein, said of her, "She has chronicled decades of America's urban life with passionate intensity using bold color applied with ever-inventive and energetic brushwork."*

184 *On November 21, 1921, an Armistice Day celebration drew thousands to Madison Square Garden. The overflow crowds poured into Madison Square Park to listen to President Harding's dedication ceremony of the Tomb of the Unknown Soldier at Arlington National Cemetery that was transmitted over the Garden's loudspeakers.*

AN END TO PAGEANTRY

The parade routes today have changed, leaving Madison Square with only a handful of festivities that bring out the bleachers along the west side of the park, the biggest of these events being the annual Gay Pride Parade and the Veterans Day Parade. (While the number of parades celebrating numerous ethnic groups has actually increased within the city, they often attract smaller fragmented crowds who are supportive of each particular event. These events take place uptown, some on upper Fifth Avenue or Broadway [for instance, the St. Patrick's Day and Thanksgiving Day Parades] and some in lower Manhattan [ticker tape parades, for example]. The annual Halloween Parade in Greenwich Village, the New Year's Eve celebration in Times Square, and the elaborate 4th

of July fireworks display on the East River come closest to evoking the spirit and excitement of the Madison Square parades and gatherings of yesteryear.)

The Veterans Day Parade appropriately culminates at Madison Square where so many of the war heroes were honored. Through the years it has drawn fewer and fewer onlookers. Mayor Ed Koch awakened a bit of old-time patriotism and excitement when he climbed aboard an air force fighter in the middle of Fifth Avenue, in the shadow of the Flatiron Building, and waved to an enthusiastic crowd. Perhaps with renewed interest in the park and its present restoration, Madison Square will become an even stronger and more meaningful venue for remembering its glorified heroes and colorful past. Alternative and innovative uses for the park, including dynamic art, music and education programs, promise to revitalize the park's appeal and set the stage as it welcomes the 21st century.

Well before the New York City Landmarks Preservation Commission was established in 1965, there was an effort to preserve some of the architectural details and sculpture of Madison Square. In the name of progress, some wonderful buildings that were once a part of the park's history were razed to make room for large corporate offices. Likewise, some of the art and sculpture were either removed or failed to withstand the test of time.

Some treasures, however, were salvaged and reinstalled on permanent exhibition in their own right or incorporated into facades of other buildings. They are now carefully looked after at the various institutions that have provided them with new homes.

* * *

THE TALLY-HO
The Museum of the
City of New York
Fifth Avenue at 103rd Street
New York City, New York

The famous carriage of Kane Delancey and the Coaching Club that initiated numerous rides from the Brunswick Hotel on Madison Square Park is now part of the Museum of the City of New York's permanent collection.

* * *

DIANA
The Philadelphia Museum of Art
Benjamin Franklin Parkway at
26th Street
Philadelphia, Pennsylvania

Diana was brought down from her Tower in 1926 upon the demolition of Madison Square Garden. At the time, she was owned by the New York Life Insurance Company, which gained title to the Garden in its declining years. Eventually New York Life presented her to the Philadelphia Museum of Art, where she is prominently displayed.

* * *

THE BASE OF THE FARRAGUT MONUMENT
The Augustus Saint-Gaudens
National Historic Site
Route 12A
Cornish, New Hampshire

By 1934 the original North River bluestone base of the Farragut Monument was in a state of deterioration, and a new pedestal was reproduced in granite. The original base was a true collaboration between Stanford White, its designer, and Saint-Gaudens, its sculptor. Saint-Gaudens not only created the intricate low relief work for White's bench-like pedestal but also sculpted the figure of Farragut. The original base was removed and reinstalled at the Augustus Saint-Gaudens National Historic Site, where it is situated on the bucolic grounds of the artist's summer home. An open, pitched-roof structure protects the base, upon which sits a reproduction of the Farragut figure cast directly from the original in Madison Square in the mid-1980s.

* * *

OLIVIA PHELPS STOKES FOUNTAIN
The Museums at Stony Brook
1208 Route 25A
Stony Brook, New York

In 1957 the Olivia Phelps Stokes Fountain was removed from Madison Square, where it had stood just outside the park's perimeter on Madison Avenue at 23rd Street. Having been warehoused and almost forgotten, the fountain was brought to the attention of a curator at the Museums at Stony Brook through an article in the *New York Times*. It was removed to Long Island and in 1990 was restored to working condition. It is now installed on the grounds of the museum.

NYMPHS AND SAYTR
Francine and Sterling Clark
Art Institute
225 South Street
Williamstown, Massachusetts

This famous and provocative painting, *Nymphs and Saytr* by Adolphe-William Bouguereau, that had hung in the Hoffman House Bar on Madison Square finally came to rest at the Francine and Sterling Clark Art Institute after a series of coincidences led Sterling Clark to this painting that he had admired as a young college student. It is now on prominent display on the first floor of the museum.

* * *

THE FACADE OF THE NATIONAL ACADEMY OF DESIGN
Our Lady of Lourdes
472 West 142nd Street
New York City, New York

With the ongoing expansion of the Metropolitan Life Insurance Company, two buildings devoted to the arts were torn down at the corner of Park Avenue and 23rd Street. They were the National Academy of Design and the Lyceum Theater. A goodly part of the facade of the National Academy was rescued and incorporated into the facade of Our Lady of Lourdes Church, located on New York's upper west side.

* * *

MADISON SQUARE PRESBYTERIAN CHURCH
The Hartford Times Building
10 Prospect Street
Hartford, Connecticut

It was thanks to Donn Barber, the architect of the Hartford Times Building, that a fair portion of the facade of the Madison Square Presbyterian Church was salvaged. The church was demolished in 1919 to make room for additional offices for the Metropolitan Life Insurance Company. Barber ingeniously incorporated the six thirty-foot pale green columns, along with windows, two balustrades and two pilasters, into the Hartford Times Building, which today is used as city offices.

* * *

DECORATIVE BALCONY FROM THE JEROME MANSION
The Brooklyn Museum of Art
200 Eastern Parkway
Brooklyn, New York

An elaborate decorative wrought-iron balcony salvaged from the Jerome Mansion, which was demolished in 1965, is in the collection of the Brooklyn Museum, though it is not currently on display.

* * *

THE FLATIRON BUILDING SCULPTURE
The Flatiron Building
175 Fifth Avenue
New York City, New York

Missing since 1991 for what was thought to be part of a restoration project, the sculpture that had once topped the Flatiron at the building's rounded point high above 23rd Street was replaced in 2001. The immense architectural detail of two figures flanking a shield served as a focal point and joined the encircling balustrade of the building's roofline. The only original physical pieces remaining were three of the four heavily tarred feet of the two figures and a section of the lower part of the shield that bore a portion of scroll work.

Although not the original, the newly fabricated sculpture will literally 'dot-the-i' on the Flatiron and park restorations, serving as a symbol of Madison Square's impressive past and its bright and vital future.

SELECTED BIBLIOGRAPHY

Armstrong, Maitland. *Day Before Yesterday, Reminiscences of a Varied Life.*
New York: Charles Scribner's Sons, 1920.

Baker, Paul R. *Stanny, The Gilded Life of Stanford White.*
New York: The Free Press, A Division of Macmillan, Inc., 1976.

Baldwin, Charles C. *Stanford White.* New York: Da Capo Press, Inc. 1976.

Baral, Robert. *Turn West on 23rd, A Toast to New York's Old Chelsea.*
New York: Fleet Publishing Corporation, 1965.

Berger, Meyer. *The Story of The New York Times, 1841–1951.*
New York: Simon and Schuster, 1951.

Boyer, Christine. *Manhattan Manners-Architecture And Style, 1850–1900.*
New York: Rizzoli International Publications, Inc., 1985.

Brown, Henry Collins. *New York in the Elegant Eighties.*
New York: Valentine's Manual, Inc., 1926.

———. *New York in the Elegant Nineties.*
Hastings-on-Hudson: Valentine's Manual, Inc., 1928.

———. *Fifth Avenue, Then and Now, 1824–1924*
(Official Publication of the Fifth Avenue Association).
New York: Wynkoop, Hallenbeck Crawford Co. 1924.

Browne, Hunius Henri. *The Great Metropolis: A Mirror of New York.*
American Publishing Company, 1869.

Burrows, Edwin G., and Mike Wallace. *Gotham, A History of New York to 1898.*
New York, Oxford: Oxford University Press, 1999.

Butler, William Allen. *A Retrospect of Forty Years, 1825–1865.*
New York: Charles Scribner's Sons, 1911.

Conrad, Peter. *The Art of the City, Views and Versions of New York.*
New York, Oxford: Oxford University Press, 1984.

Cooper-Hewitt Museum, The Smithsonian Institution's National Museum of Design.
Urban Open Spaces. New York: Rizzoli, 1981.

Dunshee, Kenneth Holcomb. *As You Pass By.*
New York: Hastings House Publishers, 1952.

Ellis, Edward *The Epic of New York City, A Narrative History.*
New York: Old Town Books, a division of Marboro Books, 1966.

Fifth Avenue Bank of New York. *Fifth Avenue Events.*
New York: Fifth Avenue Bank, 1916.

Fowler, Dorothy Ganfield. *A City Church, The First Presbyterian Church
in the City of New York 1716–1976.*
New York: The First Presbyterian Church in the City of New York, 1981.

Garmey, Stephen. *Gramercy Park: An Illustrated History of a New York Neighborhood.*
New York: Balsam Press, Inc. 1984.

Hawes, Elizabeth. *New York, New York, How the Apartment House Transformed
the Life of the City (1869–1930).*
New York: Alfred A. Knopf, 1993.

Hollander, Zander. *Madison Square Garden, A Century of Sport and Spectacle
in the World's Most Versatile State.*
New York: Hawthorn Books, Inc. 1973.

Hughes, Rupert. *The Real New York.*
New York: The Smart Set Publishing Company, 1904.

Huxtable, Ada Louise. "Grand Central Depot 1869–71."
Progressive Architecture in America (October 1956), p.135.

Jackson, Kenneth T. *The Encyclopedia of New York City.*
New York & London: Yale University Press, 1995.

Jenkins, Stephen. *The Greatest Street in The World-Broadway.*
The Story of Broadway, Old and New, from Bowling Green to Albany.
New York and London: The Knickerbocker Press, 1911.

Lamb, Martha. *History of the City of New York,* vol. 3.
New York: A. S. Barnes & Co., 1880.

Landau, Sarah Bradford, and Carl W. Condit.
Rise of the New York Skyscraper 1865–1913.
New Haven and London: Yale University Press, 1996.

Lawrence, Vera Brodsky. *Strong on Music: The New York Music Scene in the Days of
George Templeton Strong, Volume 1 Resonances 1836–1849.*
Chicago: University of Chicago Press, 1988.

Lessard, Suzannah. *The Architect of Desire.* New York: The Dial Press, 1996.

Lockwood, Charles. *Bricks & Brownstones, The New York Row House, 1783–1929.*
New York: Abbeville Press, 1972.

———. *Manhattan Moves Uptown, An Illustrated History.*
New York: Barnes and Noble, 1976.

Lowe, David Garrard. *Stanford White's New York.* New York: Doubleday, 1992.

Mayer, Gracie M. *Once Upon a City.* New York: Octagon Books, 1980.

McCabe, James D., Jr. *New York by Gaslight.* New York: Greenwich House, 1984.

McNamara, Brooks. *Day of Jubilee, The Great Age of Public Celebrations in
New York, 1788–1909.* New Jersey: Rutgers University Press, 1997.

Mendelsohn., Joyce. *Touring the Flatiron: Walks in Four Historic Districts.*
New York: New York Landmarks Conservancy, 1998.

Meriden Monographs, No. 1. *A Historical Sketch of Madison Square.*
New York: Meriden Britannia Company, 1894.

Morris, Lloyd. *Incredible New York, High Life and Low Life
of the Last Hundred Years.* New York: Random House, Inc. 1951.

New York Tribune (Saturday, November 2, 1901).

Newhall, Beaumont. *The History of Photography, from 1939 to the present.*
New York: The Museum of Modern Art, 1982.

Norton, Thomas E. *100 Years of Collecting in America,
The Story of Sotheby Parke Bernet.*
New York: Harry N. Abrams, Inc. Publishers, 1984.

Patterson, Jerry E. *Fifth Avenue, The Best Address.* New York: Rizzoli, 1998.

Picture. Issue 19, New York. Santa Fe Springs: Garener/Fulmer Lithograph, 1982.
Dorothy Norman quote on Stieglitz from Dorothy Norman.
Alfred Stieglitz: An American Seer. New York: Random House, 1973.

Pulsifer, Susan N. *A House in Time.* New York: The Citadel Press, 1958.

Roth, Leland M. *McKim, Mead and White, Architects.*
New York: Harper and Row Publishers, 1983.

Rybczynski, Witold. *A Clearing in the Distance, Frederick Law Olmsted and
America in the 19th Century.* New York: Touchstone, 1999.

Schermerhorn, Gene. *Letters to Phil, Memories of a New York Boyhood, 1848–1856.*
New York: New York Bound, 1982.

Simon, Kate. *Fifth Avenue: A Very Social History.*
New York and London: Harcourt Brace Jovanovich, 1978.

Smith, Mary Ann. "John Snook and the Design for A. T. Stewart's Store."
New York Historical Society Quarterly, vol. 58 (1974).

Stern, Robert A. M., Gregory Gilmartin, and John Massengale.
New York 1900: Metropolitan Architecture and Urbanism 1890–1915.
New York: Rizzoli, 1983.

Stern, Robert A. M., Thomas Mellins, and David Fishman. *New York 1880:
Architecture and Urbanism in the Gilded Age.*
New York: The Monacelli Press, Inc., 1999.

Stokes, I. N. Phelps. *The Iconography of Manhattan Island, 1498–1909,* 6 vols.
New York: Robert H. Dodd, 1915–26; reprinted New York: Arno, 1967.

Stokes, A. P. *Stokes Records: Notes regarding the Ancestry and Lives of Anson Phelps
Stokes and Helen Louisa (Phelps) Stokes.* New York: 1910–1915

Tales of Gaslight New York. New Jersey: Castle, 1985.

Taylor, William R. *In Pursuit of Gotham, Culture and Commerce in New York.*
New York, Oxford: Oxford University Press, 1992.

Thomas, Lately. *Delmonico's, A Century of Splendor.*
Boston: Houghton Mifflin Company, 1967.

Weitenkampf, Frank. *Manhattan Kaleidoscope.*
New York: Charles Scribner's Sons, 1947.

Wharton, Edith. *The Age of Innocence.*
New York: Charles Scribner's Sons, 1970.

White, Noval, and Elliott Willensky. *AIA Guide to New York City.*
New York: Collier Books, 1978.

Withey, Henry F., and Elsie Rathburn Withey.
Biographical Dictionary of American Architects.
Los Angeles: New Age Publishing Co., 1956.

Wolfe, Gerard R. *New York: A Guide to the Metropolis.*
New York: New York University Press, 1975.

INDEX